THIS IS NOT ANOTHER SELF-HELP BOOK

In the past few decades, there has been a flood of "self-help" books that explain the origins of unhappiness and offer varied prescriptions for "cures." But the arguments in almost all of these books are lacking in one important area—hard facts. DO YOU HAVE A DEPRESSIVE ILLNESS? is different. With well-researched information about the symptoms and causes of depression, and solid advice about proper diagnosis as well as the treatment—drugs, and the many kinds of professional therapies available—this remarkable book helps depressives and their families to recognize the warning signs of a serious depression before it becomes life-threatening. And with a detailed analysis of the treatment options, Doctors Klein and Wender point the way toward correct diagnosis and the appropriate psychological or medical help. Read on: this book could be a lifesaver.

"A very timely, much needed, beneficial book . . . filled with practical advice . . . one that will no doubt prevent much unnecessary suffering as well as save many lives."
—Artie Houston, President, National Depressive and Manic Depressive Association

DR. DONALD F. KLEIN is Professor of Psychiatry at Columbia University College of Physicians and Surgeons and Director of Research at New York State Psychiatric Institute.

DR. PAUL H. WENDER is Professor of Psychiatry and Director of Psychiatric Research at the University of Utah College of Medicine. Doctors Wender and Klein are the authors of *Mind, Mood and Medicine: A Guide to the New Biopsychiatry*, available in a Meridian edition.

Drs. Klein and Wender are both winners of the American Psychiatric Association's Prize for Psychiatric Research.

Do You Have a Depressive Illness?

How to Tell, What to Do

by

**Donald F. Klein, M.D., and
Paul H. Wender, M.D.**

A PLUME BOOK

NEW AMERICAN LIBRARY

NEW YORK AND SCARBOROUGH, ONTARIO
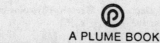

PUBLISHER'S NOTE
The ideas, procedures and
suggestions contained in this book
are not intended as a substitute
for consulting with your physician.
All matters regarding your health
require medical supervision.

Copyright © 1988 by Donald F. Klein and Paul H. Wender

SIGNET, SIGNET CLASSIC, MENTOR, ONYX, PLUME, MERIDIAN
and NAL BOOKS are published *in the United States* by
NAL PENGUIN INC., 1633 Broadway, New York, New York 10019,
in Canada by The New American Library of Canada Limited,
81 Mack Avenue, Scarborough, Ontario M1L 1M8

Library of Congress Cataloging-in-Publication Data

Klein, Donald F., 1928-
    Do you have a depressive illness? : how to tell, what to do / by
Donald F. Klein and Paul H. Wender.
        p.   cm.

    ISBN 0-452-26062-0
    1. Depression, Mental. 2. Depression, Mental—Physiological
aspects.   I. Wender, Paul H., 1934-   . II. Title.
RC537.K54 1988   88-9892
616.85'27—dc19   CIP

First Printing, August, 1988

1 2 3 4 5 6 7 8 9

PRINTED IN THE UNITED STATES OF AMERICA

AUTHORS' NOTE

Both authors contributed equally. The order of their names is an artifact of the linear nature of our language.

We have often avoided the clumsy locution "he or she" when sexual differences are not relevant. Instead, we have frequently used the pronouns at random.

The case histories are based on actual patients, but the identifying details have been changed.

D.F.K. and P.H.W.

Contents

Preface

AS PSYCHIATRISTS who have been heavily involved in research with psychiatric patients for the past twenty-five years, we have been increasingly impressed by the evidence that many severe psychiatric disorders are *illnesses*. They are often hereditary, arising from physiological malfunctions (especially in brain chemistry), and their symptoms can be lessened or eliminated by treatment with medication. We have been particularly interested in measuring the effectiveness of drug treatment, a task that involves comparisons with other treatments, including psychological therapies. This field of research is a rapidly growing one, and a striking gap has grown between what is known by clinicians and researchers and what is known by the public, even the psychologically sophisticated public. Because depressive illness, which can be devastating to individuals and their families, affects a large part of the population and does respond well to drug treatment, we think it is important to bring to the general public the most recent information on the research findings in this area.

Because of the knowledge gap, the majority of people with serious depression—most often biological depression—are not being treated adequately. It has been estimated that in the United States well over half of the people with biological depression are receiving no treatment at all, and of those who are receiving treatment, only a small portion are receiving appropriate treatment. The public has been subjected to a bewildering flood of books explaining the origins of unhappiness—including depression—and other forms of human misery. Most of these books have one thing in common: the positions they advance are not supported by scientific data. The information provided here differs in that it is supported by hard evidence that is now common knowledge among an increasingly large group of psychiatric specialists.*

One of the important components of the treatment of biological depression is education about its causes, symptoms, treatment, and outcome, and the special problems associated with it. Because biological depression is frequently chronic, it must be handled by a physician, like any other chronic disease. The most effective treatment requires that the patient be an active participant. She must learn about depression. This book is in essence a written version of the "course" we give to the depressed patients we treat. It is a product of what we have learned, including what our patients have taught us.

---

*In an earlier book for the general public we summarized the scientific evidence on the origin and treatment of many psychiatric disorders: Paul H. Wender and Donald F. Klein, *Mind, Mood, and Medicine* (New York: New American Library, 1982). The scientific evidence for the effectiveness of drug therapy is reviewed in Donald F. Klein et al., *Diagnosis and Drug Treatment of Psychiatric Disorders* (Baltimore: Williams & Wilkins, 1980).

CHAPTER
1 What Is Biological Depression?

IF YOU HAVE picked up this book and are reading this sentence, there is a good chance that you are worried about depression in yourself or others in your family. That is not an idle concern, since undiagnosed and untreated depression can have serious consequences. Most serious depression requires medical treatment and therefore is a medical problem, even though it may be precipitated or worsened by psychological factors. Correct medical diagnosis should lead to a treatment that in most instances is effective, fast, and inexpensive.

Depression and manic-depression are among the most common biological disorders seen in psychiatry. One woman in five and one man in ten can expect to develop a depression or manic-depression sometime during the course of their lives. In other words, one person in seven can expect to develop depression or manic-depression during his or her lifetime—in total, well over thirty million of the current U.S. population.

At least ten percent of people who develop depressive or manic-depressive illness will commit suicide—over three million of the current population. Suicide is the eighth leading cause of death in adults and is the second leading cause of death in children and adolescents (often through apparent accidents). The ability to recognize depressive illness in yourself or loved ones may be a matter of life and death.

Suicide is obviously the most serious outcome, but even when depression does not kill, it often destroys families and careers. Failure to treat depressive illness leads to personal, familial, and social disasters. A particularly vivid statement of what it means to be severely depressed comes from Russell Hampton's autobiography, *The Far Side of Despair* (1975):

> If there were a physical disease that manifested itself in some particularly ugly way, such as pustulating sores or a sloughing off of the flesh accompanied by pain of an intense and chronic nature, readily visible to everyone, and if that disease affected fifteen million people in our country, and further, if there were virtually no help or succor for most of these persons, and they were forced to walk among us in their obvious agony, we would rise up as one social body in sympathy and anger. We would give of our resources, both human and economic, and we would plead and demand that this suffering be eased. There isn't such a physical disease, but there is such a disease of the mind, and about fifteen million people around us are suffering from it. But we have not risen in anger and sympathy, although they are walking among us and crying in their pain and anguish.

Depressive illness is common, painful, and dangerous, but since Russell Hampton wrote that passage, treatments for depression have been developed that yield excellent results. How can we make sure that people do get proper treatment? First they must be taught to recognize the warning symptoms of depressive illness, just as they have been taught to detect the warning symptoms of cancer. People are not expected to diagnose cancer, but they can learn to watch for suggestive symptoms by, for example, examining their breasts for lumps and being alert for sores that do not heal or moles that change color. Learning to observe these bodily changes is a medical early-warning system. The prospective patient is in a better position to find *possible* early signs than the doctor is. Usually such symptoms are not signs of cancer. But if they are, they will have been detected early—and the cancer will be more treatable. In the same way, we want people who read this book to be able to recognize the early symptoms of depression. We want to teach them a psychiatric early-warning system so that they can get treatment for themselves or someone close to them before the danger has mounted.

People know when they are sad, of course, and understandably they do not think of that feeling—and the related feeling called "depression"—as an illness. However, two distinct states of emotion are commonly confused when people refer to depression. Sadness, everyday psychological depression, is a normal human reaction, a normal response to loss, a feeling associated with grief; depressive illness—for which we also use the term *biological depression*—is a disease, a medical condition. Depressive illness can be insidious because it frequently resembles the kind of unhappiness that is a normal part of human living. Without help, most people cannot distinguish between psychological depression and biological depressive illness. One reason is that most people, when depressed, immediately trace their emotional state to problems in their current or past life, failing to recognize distinctive clues hinting that they may instead be suffering from a disease. Another reason is that biological depression can be triggered by life events, so that normal grief is intensified to a state recognizable as pathological grief.

People must learn not only how to recognize biological depression but also whom to contact when they suspect they are suffering from it. This is important for both diagnosis and treatment. Although many psychiatrists are now able to diagnose and treat biological depression, many other mental health professionals, such as psychologists and social workers, cannot treat it as fully because the optimum treatment may involve the use of medication; only physicians can prescribe antidepressant medication. The evidence is compelling that effective medical treatment can relieve or totally remove the symptoms in eighty percent of people with severe depression. The antidepressant medications are not habit-forming or abusable. Research studies have shown that the administration of antidepressants in normal subjects produces certain side effects, but no feeling of euphoria. Moreover, there is stronger evidence that they are not abusable. In the thirty years that they have been available, they have never been sold on the street.

In urging treatment of depressive disease by medication, we are not ignoring the possible usefulness of psychotherapy. However, we believe that prescription of antidepressant medication should almost always be the first step. During the initial phase of treatment psychotherapy may also be helpful in maintaining the patient's morale, giving him a reassuring perspective on his future and ensuring that he continues to take his medication. Following relief of symptoms through the use of medication, psychotherapy may be able to alleviate many of the residual psychological symptoms.

One last point: this is not another self-help book. Our overriding message is that certain forms of depression *cannot* be overcome by self-help. They require medical evaluation and medical treatment. The purpose of the book is to enable the layperson to recognize the *symptoms* of biological depression and to know *when* and *where* to seek help, how the illness is properly *evaluated* and *treated*, what to expect from treatment, and what to expect when the course of therapy is over.

This book does not in itself provide a solution to the problem of biological depression. Its aim is to provide the sufferers and their families with the information necessary to seek appropriate professional help and to understand the illness. It will serve its purpose if it enables those who are depressed to realize that they are afflicted with an illness, not an unchangeable reaction to life's injustices, hardships, griefs, and misfortunes. In that way they can better understand what is happening to them and how they can take steps to obtain effective treatment for their condition.

CHAPTER

2 Symptoms of Mood Disorders: Recognizing Biological Depression

DEPRESSIVE ILLNESS is a disease. As with any other disease, the physician—the psychiatrist—has guidelines and rules for making the diagnosis. The rules used for diagnosing depressive illness are simple. They depend on the presence or absence of symptoms that anyone can recognize. The layman can use these rules to rate himself and come to a rough conclusion:

I probably do have a depressive illness;
I might have a depressive illness; or
I don't have a depressive illness.

The words "might" and "probably" are used because determining how severe a symptom is—or isn't—is a judgment call. The skilled psychiatrist's expertness involves the ability to judge the seriousness of a person's symptoms. This judgment is based on experience with many patients and includes the ability to judge not only what a person says but how he says it. The psychiatrist uses a systematic interview to evaluate what a depressed person tells him. This can be used to fill out a comprehensive rating scale and is more accurate than giving people questionnaires.

Just as one would not diagnose and treat a mole that changes color or a sore that does not heal, one cannot self-diagnose and treat depression. In both cases self-examination enables a person to determine whether he or she should get professional advice about treatment. We will present the psychiatrist's rating scale in the form of questions that someone might be asked during an evaluation interview. After using the rating scale, go on to the fuller description of the symptoms and brief histories describing how these symptoms have appeared—or have been hidden—in patients we have treated. In elaborating the symptoms of depression we will include symptoms that are not part of our initial self-rating questionnaire but are commonly found among depressed persons. This extended description plus examples from actual patients will provide a clearer understanding of what we mean by vague terms such as "loss of pleasure" and "loss of energy." We will also describe the symptoms of mania, a paradoxical form of depression commonly known as manic-depression.

We want to emphasize again that this is not a self-help book that will teach people to diagnose themselves. We want to help people learn the warning signals so that they can decide whether to get a diagnosis from a qualified professional. Individuals (sometimes aided by their families or others close to them) are in the best possible position to detect changes—possibly dangerous ones—in themselves. The questions and methods of scoring follow. (For rating someone close to you rather than yourself, think how the scale might apply to that person.)

Depression Self-Rating Scale

Have either of the following symptoms been present nearly every day for *at least two weeks?*

A.1. Have you been sad, blue, or "down in the dumps"?

A.2. Have you lost interest or pleasure in all or almost all the things you usually do (work, hobbies, other activities)?

If *either* A.1 *or* A.2 is true, continue. If not, you probably do not have a depressive illness.

Have any of the following been present nearly every day for *at least two weeks*?

B. Loss of energy, easy fatigability,
    tiredness?   NO   YES
    Poor appetite *or* weight loss *or*
    increased appetite *or* weight gain?   NO   YES
    Sleep difficulty (insomnia) *or*
    sleeping too much?   NO   YES
    Restlessness (mental, physical)
    or clear-cut slowing down physically?   NO   YES
    Decreased sexual drive or pleasure?   NO   YES
    Feelings of self-reproach, excessive
    guilt, or worthlessness?   NO   YES
    Slowing of thinking, poor concentration,
    indecisiveness?   NO   YES
    Thoughts of death, thoughts of committing suicide,
    wishing you were dead?   NO   YES

If A.1 or A.2 is true, and if you answer "yes" to any four of these eight questions, you probably have a depressive illness and should consult a qualified professional. Even if you have only two or more you should consider a checkup. (How to find help is discussed in Chapter 5.) One reason we say that you *probably* have a depressive illness is that some people with these symptoms have a physical illness such as anemia or low thyroid activity. When you seek professional help for a possible depressive illness, it is important that your physician makes sure that you have a complete physical checkup at the same time.

The psychiatrist will also try to determine whether you may be going through a temporary upset due to life circumstances and do not really have a biological depression.

In deciding whether or not you have depressive illness, you should try not to give too much weight to what may seem to you to be plausible reasons for your bad feelings. Life is never perfect, and if people look hard enough, they can find some reason for feeling bad. Even a major loss, such as a death in the family or a divorce, may not be the real reason for your depressed emotional state. Furthermore, depressive illness itself may make people less capable of dealing with life's problems and can actually cause such life stresses as loss of jobs and breakups in relationships. In such instances what looks like the cause of depression may actually be one of its results. Depressive illness is often triggered by a real event but still requires treatment.

Depressive illnesses are easiest to recognize when someone has a sudden change in his or her emotional state for no apparent reason. People who find themselves saying, "I can't understand why I feel so bad. There is no good reason for it," *always* need a diagnostic review. However, depressive illnesses may develop gradually, so that the patient doesn't see any big difference between his current emotional state and how he felt a few years ago. Such a person may think his depressed mood is simply his normal state—he is just a down character. Such constant depressed conditions also often respond to medical treatment.

One rule of thumb involves the length of the period of distress and the degree of trouble that it has produced. If the distress has lasted for over a month, or if family, employment, or social life has been substantially affected, a checkup is highly advisable. However, even those who have been feeling apathetic for only a few weeks, or who can handle their usual activities only by great effort, should also consider a checkup.

There are several sorts of depressive illness, and there are many different degrees of severity. As we indicated, someone with depressive illness may not manifest all of the above symptoms. Nonetheless, if some of these symptoms are all too familiar, you should not put off getting help.

Therefore, rate yourself on the symptoms with an open mind. If you find that you may have a depressive illness, you should get a checkup, regardless of any social or psychological explanations that occur to you.

In order to provide a better picture of how symptoms of these kinds affect people's lives, we shall present a series of disguised excerpts from case histories of patients we have treated. Each of these patients represents a different variety of depression. We shall begin by briefly describing each patient, and will then indicate how the symptoms manifested themselves in their lives.

Illustrative Patients:

Jill Jason. A busy young housewife and mother who usually enjoys a variety of activities at home and in the community.

Mary Stenn. A vivacious young receptionist who loves dating and romance and has had a long string of boyfriends.

Milton Meyer. A skillful surgeon in his forties who ordinarily enjoys not only his profession but also gardening and playing the violin.

Bob Rush. A successful producer of Broadway shows who usually finds his life exciting and fulfilling.

Saul Schwartz. A middle-aged businessman who usually finds his work and his family sources of satisfaction.

Marge Pearl. A wealthy, middle-aged housewife who normally has an active social life and good family relationships.

Ralph White. A young man who has been an outstanding high school student, captain of the football team, and near the top of his class.

John White. Ralph's father, a prosperous sales manager who handles his demanding job very responsibly.

Mike Green. An expert technician who has performed his work well for many years.

George Harris. A fifty-one-year-old high-middle management executive in a large corporation whose marriage has just fallen apart.

Carl Davis. A thirty-one-year-old computer repairman whose work has been impaired by a hand injury.

Edith Forbes. A fifty-year-old married professional woman who has had symptoms of "neurotic" depression for ten years.

Aaron Baker. An energetic investment consultant who sometimes develops highly creative ideas for new investment possibilities.

The Patients' Problems

Loss of Interest

The symptoms of sadness and loss of interest refer to two highly important aspects of depressive illness. Most people who are depressed will say they are sad or blue or down in the dumps. In addition, many will say that they have lost interest in everything. A few people with a depressive illness are not sad or blue but instead have widespread loss of interest in their usual pursuits. These people may not recognize themselves as depressed, but this symptom is a critical one.

People have a wide variety of interests and pleasures in their lives—including, usually, simple biological pleasures such as eating and sex. People also look forward to family gatherings, sports, vacations, social activities, hobbies, and, in general, to the possibility that good things will be happening. When they think of future pleasant events, they usually have a sense of warm, optimistic hopefulness that is itself already a pleasant feeling.

Many depressed people lose these warm feelings and experience a sharp decrease in the ability to have pleasure. Activities that normally excite them are boring or unrewarding. Good food may taste like cardboard; they just peck at their meals. There is a loss of sexual desire and responsivity. Formerly satisfactory sexual relationships become unstimulating and burdensome. They feel apathetic and unreactive, and may have a diminished capacity for closeness with others.

Normal mood varies, depending on circumstances. Rewarding lives result in animated, outgoing moods. If things turn sour, then mood becomes subdued, cautious, and somewhat indifferent. When things go well again, the usual good feeling is restored.

Depressed people are different from people whose unhappiness is an obviously appropriate response to life circumstances. The mood of a depressed person is not in tune with the environment. Some severely depressed people are utterly unresponsive to what are usually thought of as good parts of life. It is not uncommon for depressed people to be told that they need a vacation or a change only to find that even when they go on a trip that they may have planned years in advance, they continue to feel bad.

Other depressed people can be temporarily cheered up. They will often crave attention and social stimulation because that is the only way they can bring their mood up to normal. However, what marks them as having an illness is the fact that without continued excitement and praise, their mood slumps down again.

Jill Jason found herself increasingly indifferent about her usual activities. She stopped going to her bridge club, was bored by television, was unsympathetic to her husband's difficulties and triumphs, and just went through the motions with the children. She complained, "I don't know what's gotten into me. Everything was going so well. Now I don't give a damn, and I can't snap out of it. My son came home with all A's on his report card and I couldn't care less."

Jill's mood was particularly bad in the morning. Sometimes late at night she got a kick out of watching television. But by the next morning, everything seemed awful again. Her husband began to complain that she never enjoyed anything anymore, that even her sense of humor had disappeared.

When a doctor told Jill that she had been working too hard and needed a change of scene, she went to a resort with her husband. However, the vacation was a total disaster. Jill participated in a few activities and then stopped going altogether. She spent most of the time sitting in their room. She let her husband drag her to the swimming pool a few times because she had always loved to swim, but now she got nothing out of it.

Mary Stenn had had a series of unexpected disappointments and found herself less interested in going out. She spent more and more time alone. She told her friends that life was a rat race and that she was growing up. However, she was also losing interest in her work.

Mary was at her best in the morning. She would get up, cook breakfast, and get to work by 8:30 A.M. At that time she enjoyed applying herself and solving problems. However, by mid-afternoon she knew that she was just shuffling papers around. By the time she was ready to leave the office in the evening, she could accomplish nothing.

Mary spent a lot of time quietly in bed. However, when friends came over she would brighten and become animated. Frequently they tried to talk her into going to a party, to cheer her up. She usually refused, saying that parties were dull and there wasn't any point to them.

Surprisingly, when she did agree to go out, she seemed to have fun and was almost her old self. But when she got home she slumped into her low mood again. After one of these experiences, when her friends tried to persuade her to go to another party, she said that she wouldn't go because parties were boring. Her friends reminded her that she had seemed to enjoy the last party, but Mary insisted that she really didn't feel up to it.

Finally, like Jill Jason, Mary was persuaded to go to a resort for a change. At first it seemed like the right prescription. She danced, played tennis, met some new attractive men, and exchanged phone numbers. Her old zest for life seemed to return. However, when she went back to the city her level of interest slowly declined. She didn't call her new friends, and when they called her, she saw them a few times but then let the relationships fizzle out.

Milton Meyer was not only a successful surgeon but also enjoyed teaching and was an avid amateur violinist and an enthusiastic gardener. Long before he noticed anything unusual, his wife observed gradual changes. His interest in surgery lessened and he disparaged his work, saying that it was not very useful in the long run, that it only patched things up. He found reasons for avoiding teaching, stopped playing in his amateur quartet, and hired someone to take care of his garden. His wife sensed his increasing withdrawal, but when she asked him whether he was depressed, he denied it. In terms of how he felt, he was being honest. He was not sad, blue, or down in the dumps—he had just lost interest in everything.

Loss of Energy

Most of the time people have a feeling of zest, of get up and go. When things interest them, they feel energized and will pursue their goals actively. Depressed people feel as if they have run out of gas. They complain about fatigue, feel that everything is an effort, that they just can't get going, that their body feels heavy or leaden, that they are listless and slowed down. They find themselves unable to achieve their usual goals.

Jill Jason started to complain that she was weary all the time. She was usually efficient and well organized, but now she procrastinated with her work, putting off tasks that had to be done around the house. Because of her lack of interest and lack of energy, she became progressively withdrawn socially. When her friends told her that she needed vitamins or a tonic, she tried them, but they didn't help.

Mary Stenn expected to hear from her remaining boyfriend one Friday about weekend plans, but he didn't call. Suddenly she was overcome by overwhelming fatigue. Her body felt made of lead. Previously she had been uninterested in making a special effort to engage in various activities, but now she felt physically incapable of moving. She crawled into bed, where she spent the entire weekend eating Oreos.

Appetite and Weight Disturbances: Changes in Eating Patterns

For most people, food is one of the greatest pleasures. It is common knowledge that appetite disturbances accompany all sorts of illnesses. This seems particularly true of depressions. Some people eat more when depressed, and some eat less.

Mary Stenn spent a great deal of time at home alone as she became more withdrawn. She watched television and ate junk food. She had a particularly strong craving for sweets, carbohydrates, and chocolate. She gained fifteen pounds, which added to her feelings of self-disgust and her unwillingness to try to be socially active. At times she would stuff herself with so much candy that she would force herself to throw up to relieve her bloating. Mary had read some pop psychology that told her that she was acting infantile because eating was the only way she could feel loved.

Jill Jason, in contrast, just pecked at her food. She said that nothing tasted good and ignored even her favorite dishes. Her husband told her that she would get really sick if she didn't eat, so she would make a real effort to get something down every day. To her, eating was a chore, and at times she just couldn't do it. She was getting very thin.

Sleep Disturbances

People differ in their need for sleep and their sleep pattern. Temporary difficulties in falling asleep, particularly when under tension, are common. Some people have various patterns of broken sleep referred to as insomnia. Many depressives fall asleep with ease only to have restless sleep and early-morning awakening. Others seem to require remarkably large amounts of sleep. Although it is clear that not everyone with sleep irregularities is depressed, changes in sleep patterns frequently accompany depression and are a vital warning sign.

Jill Jason, although fearful and upset, had little difficulty falling asleep. As a matter of fact, she welcomed sleep since it gave her some relief. Nevertheless, she would awaken several times in the middle of the night and feel awful. Her gloom and feelings of hopelessness were at their worst. After much tossing and turning, she would eventually fall back to sleep. Finally, at five in the morning

she would awaken and find it impossible to go back to
sleep even though she felt exhausted.

Mary Stenn, as she became less and less interested in her
life, was sleeping more and more. When working, she had
waves of fatigue and sleepiness that prevented her from
doing her job properly. Finally she quit work and stayed at
home, where she took frequent naps or simply dozed in
bed all day. She explained her behavior by saying she was
retreating from reality.

Other Physical Symptoms

Periods of pain and bodily distress are usually signs of
illness. Most such difficulties are temporary, and people
usually shrug them off or take it easy for a while until they
go away. If sufficiently distressed they may seek medical
attention.

The tendency to seek medical attention is quite variable.
Some people consider it a sign of weakness to seek help or
to complain, so they minimize their difficulties and dis-
comfort in a stoical way. Others find their distress too
difficult to bear alone and frequently turn to friends, family, clergy, or doctors for help.

Most people can't stand the idea that they may have a
disturbance of their emotions or feelings, since they think
that would label them as crazy. Therefore, when they are
in distress they find it far easier to believe that something
is physically wrong with them than to recognize that they
are having emotional problems.

Jill Jason's husband was losing patience. He finally told
her that if she didn't go to her family doctor he would drag
her there. Jill then told him that she thought she might
have cancer. She had all these weak feelings and was
losing weight. Every once in a while she felt funny all over,
as if she might faint. She had been brooding about the

possibility of cancer for several months but was afraid to mention it because that might make it come true. She was afraid to find out what the doctor might discover.

When she finally went for a physical examination, her doctor found no signs of cancer or any other physical illness. Although she was obviously haggard, underweight, and miserable, he told her that there was nothing wrong with her and that she should buck up, pull herself together, and stop feeling so sorry for herself. On the way home, Jill said that she still thought she had cancer and that the doctor had missed it.

Mary Stenn thought that she had heart disease. Every once in a while her heart would go a mile a minute, and she would feel as if her head was floating off her shoulders and that she might fall down any second. Several times she had such difficulty in catching her breath that she thought she was dying and went to an emergency room. They told her that her heart was fine and it was just her nerves.

One doctor suggested that she take tranquilizers for her panics, and, after much hesitation, she took some. They seemed slightly helpful, but she was still weary, fatigued, and socially isolated; occasionally she again thought she was having a heart attack. Her family thought she was playing for sympathy.

Bob Rush, for no apparent reason, developed a low-grade, chronic bellyache. Sometimes he would feel as if he had diarrhea and would suddenly have to rush to the bathroom. He found himself so preoccupied with this that he was not doing justice to the theatrical enterprises he was producing. Wherever he went, the first thing he would do was check out where the bathroom was. He began to avoid long trips. His social life became progressively more constricted as he made excuses not to go to places where he would not have ready access to a bathroom.

Bob went to many different doctors, who all told him that there was nothing wrong with his physical health and that he was being silly. He began to feel sad and withdrawn but blamed this on his physical troubles.

Saul Schwartz said there was nothing wrong with him even though he hadn't worked for the past two months. He didn't see what all the fuss was about because it was his terrible backache that kept him from working. The doctor had told him that he couldn't find anything wrong with his back and that he was sure the pain would go away in time. Saul was simply waiting for the pain to go away. His married son, David, kept telling him that something must be wrong besides his back because he wasn't even reading the newspapers anymore and he had gotten very quiet.

David was worried because when he persuaded his father to come out for a ride or to go to the movies, Saul didn't enjoy himself. Who would enjoy themselves if they had a bad back? Saul had never been a complainer and he wasn't complaining now. He didn't even talk about his back. He only mentioned it when people told him he should be trying to do more. Saul's wife asked him whether he was depressed, because he seemed so blue and quiet. Saul said that he wasn't sad or blue but was just quiet because of his back.

Decreased Sexual Drive

As *Jill Jason* steadily lost interest in her usual activities, she showed less enthusiasm for sexual intercourse. Her husband sensed that she seemed to feel that their previously enjoyable sexual relationship had now become an unpleasant chore.

Restlessness or Slowing Down: Changes in Movement and Speech Patterns

Everyone has an individual pattern of speech and motion. Some people are quiet, whereas others talk a lot. Some people are active and restless, while others can sit contentedly for long periods. Depressive illness often markedly changes these patterns.

Jill Jason was getting quieter and quieter and more and more immobile. Her family would find her sitting for hours in a chair, looking blankly at the wall. When they asked her how she was feeling, she seemed at first not to hear them, but after a marked delay she spoke a few words in a weak voice. She said nothing spontaneously. Her family thought she just wanted to be left alone, so they left her alone.

Marge Pearl couldn't stop talking or pacing. As her husband came through the door, she assailed him with complaints about herself, about him, about the neighbors and the family. She felt so bad that he had to do something immediately because she just couldn't go on like this. She nervously paced around the apartment wringing her hands and picking at her cuticles. At times she got so upset that she pulled her hair out.

Self-Reproach and Guilt (Low Self-Esteem and Painful Mood and Thought Content)

Low self-esteem is usually not recognized as one of the most common symptoms of depression. On the whole, most people think well of themselves. Most people know that they are not extraordinarily charming, not strikingly handsome or beautiful, not brilliant or talented, but they are satisfied with themselves anyway. They can usually think of something they're good at and somebody who wants to be with them. Despite current popular ideas to the contrary—fostered by television talk shows, movies, books, and magazines—most people are optimistic and adaptable, even under difficult circumstances.

If someone has failed to reach his goals, or has been rejected or put down by loved ones, that may result in temporary bad feelings about himself. But such feelings rarely last long, and they usually force the person into some form of constructive activity.

Since depressed people view the future pessimistically and are unable to respond positively, even to good news and stimulating activities, it is not surprising that many conclude that it is all their fault and they are ineffectual losers. Such feelings are often explained psychologically on the grounds that such people must have been treated badly by their parents, who left them with permanent psychological scars.

The wretched mood that characterizes depressives is often accompanied by negative emotions and thoughts about themselves. They may brood about their failures and feel worthless and self-deprecatory. These feelings may become so painful that the depressed person simply cannot stand himself and is plagued by thoughts of guilt over past failures. He begins to feel that he is being punished and should expect punishment, and that perhaps he would be better off dead.

The intense painfulness of many depressions is difficult for the ordinary person to appreciate. Therefore, when a depressed person tries to communicate about how bad he feels, he is often criticized because it looks like some sort of act or put-on.

Jill Jason told her husband that she thought she was a terrible person and a failure as a mother and wife, and then she cried bitterly. Initially sympathetic, her husband told her that he loved her, that the whole family loved her, and that everyone thought she was a wonderful person. At first this seemed to help her, but the next day she felt as bad as ever and complained constantly again.

After a while Jill's husband became thoroughly irritated. No matter what he said or did, it didn't work, leaving him feeling helpless and overwhelmed. At times he got quite angry at her. "Why are you behaving this way? You've had everything anyone should want." He couldn't help feeling that his wife was like a bottomless pit that nothing could fill.

Poor Concentration and Indecisiveness: Mental Difficulties

Many people have small fluctuations in their ability to concentrate. When fatigued, they find it more difficult to concentrate and to stay focused. Depressed people have many complaints about their mental functioning. They feel that their memory is shot and that they cannot pay attention. In addition, they often behave in an extremely indecisive and perplexed fashion, as if they just can't figure things out.

Most non-impulsive people deliberate carefully about major decisions, such as whether to accept or quit a job, or whether or not to get married. Indecisiveness is a symptom of depression when individuals cannot make up their minds about relatively trivial matters. An example would be a woman who is about to go out to dinner with friends but who delays the group's departure for half an hour because she cannot decide whether she wants to eat at a French or Italian restaurant.

Jill Jason had been the mainstay of her church group. When a social event or dinner had to be arranged, she was a take-charge, get-it-done person. Now when she was asked to organize a church supper, she felt completely overwhelmed. She couldn't decide whether she should do it or not and kept wavering back and forth. When her husband told her with exasperation that she had managed such events ten times before without trouble, she stared at him blankly and started to cry helplessly. Jill's husband told the church group that she couldn't do it, hoping that she would feel less burdened, but that didn't help, either. She persisted in feeling overwhelmed, incompetent, and indecisive.

Deterioration of Social Relationships

Most people have a network of friends and family members whom they depend on for help when trouble strikes.

People often have little informal mutual-aid societies and get much of their joy in life from their friends and lovers. Depression sabotages these relationships, so that family and longtime friends begin to drift away.

Jill Jason had stopped going to bridge parties. At first her friends came to visit, but she was silent and unresponsive. When they would joke with her, trying to cheer her up, she didn't crack a smile. When they told her that she'd be all right soon, she just shook her head. She didn't return their calls and visits, and after a while they rarely called. Her husband started to stay out late after work because her dissatisfaction with everything made him feel helpless and frustrated.

Mary Stenn still enjoyed her relationship with her boyfriend. Because that was the only real source of pleasure that she still had, she became very greedy and demanding about it. When her boyfriend told her that he would call her at 9:00 P.M. but called at 9:15 because his train had been delayed, she burst into tears and told him that he couldn't treat her so cruelly. He should know how bad she felt and how much she looked forward to seeing him and how her whole life depended on him and his love for her, and where would she be without him? Under such pressure he eventually stopped seeing her.

Marge Pearl got nasty. She told her husband that it was all his fault that she felt so terrible and that everyone had let her down. She complained incessantly that nobody loved her or wanted her or paid any attention to her. After a while she was right.

For both Mary and Marge, depression led to increased demands that could not be satisfied and drove others away. Jill's unresponsiveness had the same effect.

Increased Use of Intoxicants and Drugs

Alcohol and more recently marijuana are commonly consumed for recreational purposes. Most people can use these substances in moderation without too much difficulty. However, many people are unable to control their consumption of liquor and drugs, developing patterns of overuse that may destroy their lives.

Why some people can remain social drinkers while others become alcoholics is not fully understood. At least part of the answer is that some are suffering from depression and are using alcohol or marijuana as mental anesthetics and temporary distractions. They are really attempting to medicate themselves. However, because these substances do not lift the depression, they increase their consumption of them in their search for relief.

Marge Pearl's husband was astonished one night when he came home to find Marge drunk. He and Marge often had a couple of drinks, but the only time he had ever seen her drunk was after a big New Year's Eve party. He certainly didn't think that she ever drank during the day.

When Marge sobered up she told him that she had just felt so bad that day, so lonely and isolated, that she thought maybe a little drink would help her out, and indeed it did. However, she hadn't expected to polish off the whole bottle. She said she wouldn't do it again, but she did, and increasingly often.

Ralph White was the pride of his family. He was captain of the high school football team and near the top of his class. Everyone knew that Ralph had a big future ahead of him. Then Ralph's marks began to slip. He said that it was hard for him to concentrate, but actually he was spending less time at his studies. His teammates started to complain about him because his judgment on the field seemed impaired. He called the wrong plays and didn't respond rapidly when the other team tried something new.

Ralph began to hang out with a different crowd, who used drugs. He began to use marijuana steadily and started to cut classes. The school principal finally called his parents in and told them sadly that Ralph seemed to have a drug problem.

Vocational Failure

In the same way that Ralph White dramatically manifested a loss of competence in his school activities, prosperous businessmen and hardworking professionals may also suddenly become ineffective.

John White, Ralph's father, was upset about his son's difficulties. He felt that somehow he had let Ralph down and was to blame. At work he became lost in guilty ruminations. Previously decisive and energetic, he now had trouble making up his mind about everything. His co-workers, who depended on him, became very dissatisfied, and finally his boss told him that he'd better snap out of it.

John tried without success to return to his previous level of functioning. He knew that brooding about Ralph's difficulties did his son no good and wasn't helping him, either, but he just couldn't stop it. He was starting to wake up at night, and his appetite was going down.

Hostility and Irritability

Some people think that an inability to express anger causes depression. They even argue that depression is anger turned back against oneself. This particular theory ignores the fact that when in the midst of depressive periods, many people are far more irritable and angry than usual. Moreover, the irritability may get worse when such people suspect that they may be having emotional problems but are not yet ready to admit it.

John White had always been easy to work for. He rarely snapped at anyone, and even when he had to chastise one of his salesmen for goofing off, he always did it in a straightforward way. He didn't angrily bawl out the salesman but simply tried to change his bad habits and improve his productivity.

Lately, however, John White was barking at everyone. Even the slightest error, of no real consequence, provoked a tirade. His secretary of twenty years finally told him that he was causing a lot of trouble. She was shocked when he told her to shut up and mind her own business.

Marge Pearl was becoming impossible to live with. Everything caused an argument. She was upset when her children didn't visit and berated them over the phone. When they did visit, she yelled at them for not visiting more often.

Marge fired her longtime maid, accusing her of getting uppity. She fired the next maid because she couldn't learn fast enough where things were. She fired still another maid because she didn't like her expression. She spent a lot of time talking about how you can't get decent help anymore. When she and her husband went to restaurants she often got into embarrassing fights with the waiters, saying the food was never any good. Her continued excessive drinking made her temper even worse.

Marge's husband, Bob, told her that he thought that something was definitely wrong with her. She used to be so sweet and helpful, but now she complained about others all the time. Marge said that she had every reason to complain because she had discovered how lousy everyone was, including her husband. Look at the way her so-called friends had stopped calling her.

When Bob dragged Marge to the family doctor, the doctor said that there wasn't anything obviously wrong with her but since she had felt so bad for a year now, maybe she ought to see a colleague of his for a consultation. When Marge asked what the colleague's specialty was, the doctor answered that she was a nerve doctor.

"You think I'm crazy," yelled Marge. "No," said the doctor, "I just think you might need a little help in getting yourself together." "You want to put me away," Marge whimpered. "I'm crazy." "Look, Marge," said the doctor, "we just want you to talk with somebody for a while. It will help you feel better."

Marge said that she would think about it, but she didn't go.

Distortion of Reality

Our moods color our understanding of the world and ourselves. When we feel down, the world seems less satisfactory, and we seem less admirable. When we are up, the world is an interesting place, and we think we're pretty good. Depression causes major distortions in our perception of reality, and therefore makes handling our problems even more difficult.

John White went into a real funk when his boss told him that he better snap out of it. He finally told the boss that he was quitting because he couldn't stand letting everyone down. The boss was astonished. He told John that he only meant that John should get some help. He added that John had been one of his best workers for many years, and he certainly had no intention of firing him. John repeated that he just wasn't up to it; thinking that he would surely be fired soon, he stopped coming to work.

Dealing with the Future: Hopelessness, Suicidal Thoughts, and Suicide Attempts

When normal people think about the future, their feelings are a mixture of pluses and minuses. When they think about past happy events or imagine pleasant future possibilities, they have positive, warm feelings of recollection or anticipation. Many of us spend a lot of time daydreaming, which is nothing more than making ourselves feel good by thinking that the future might work out in ways that we would like. Such daydreams are often constructive since thinking about possibilities that produce good feelings may stir one into related realistic activity. This is what we mean by saying that a person is in a hopeful frame of mind and acting in an enterprising way.

When people think about past unhappy events and possible future difficulties, their mood changes to tenseness and apprehension. However, sometimes when they perceive trouble coming and feel anxious about it, they are also stirred into useful action. They think about possible maneuvers that will prevent the trouble from occurring or will at least remove them from the scene of probable pain. Once people have figured out a good strategy for avoiding impending trouble, their sense of hopefulness returns and they attempt to carry out their protective plans.

The depressed person has a marked decrease in the ability to remember and imagine pleasantly. When he thinks about the future or the past, all he focuses on are the minuses. The pluses don't get through or are greatly reduced. Therefore, depressed persons cannot feel pleasant hopefulness.

A severe inability to feel optimism may lead to suicide. Since our attempts to deal with the future are steered by our hopeful thinking, the depressed person's loss of hope prevents him from planning constructively. He feels overwhelmed and helpless. When this feeling becomes too painful, many depressed people feel they would be better off dead. They would no longer be a burden to their family and they would no longer have to suffer such pain. Sometimes when they express such feelings, family and friends tend not to take them seriously. It is commonly thought that people who talk about suicide don't actually take their own lives, but this is wrong.

Mike Green thought that he was a total failure. Although he had been an expert technician for many years, he became convinced that the new technology was just getting too difficult. He quit work and stayed home, brooding and spending much of his time in solitary drinking. One day he told his wife that he would be better off dead. Frightened, she insisted that he see a doctor.

Mike told the doctor that he was just kidding and that being out of work would upset anybody. The doctor suggested that Mike take a tranquilizer.

A few days later, Mike's wife came home from a trip to the grocery store and found him hanging from a basement beam. His suicide note said that it wasn't her fault but he knew that for him the future was hopeless.

Depressive Reactions to Threatening Life Events

The patients described above, despite their differences, all have in common depressive symptoms that are not clearly related to disastrous life events. In the two examples below, the depressions followed unfortunate life circumstances. Nevertheless, these depressions differ qualitatively from each other, as will be shown in the section on treatment of the illustrative patients.

George Harris came to the University Depression Clinic to participate in a study comparing the effects of placebo, a standard antidepressant, and an experimental antidepressant. For several years his marriage had been deteriorating, and a few months earlier his foreign-born wife had informed him that she planned to return to her native country, taking their fourteen-year-old daughter and as much of their money as she could get. Shortly thereafter, his corporation had decided to reduce output by seventy-five percent. George would be laid off, receiving only a few months pay. His management job was so specialized that he doubted whether he could find another like it.

At the first interview, the psychiatrist saw a middle-aged man whose lined face and slow-moving, bent-over posture reflected his inner state. In a voice filled with tears he described his marital and vocational disasters. The symptoms were typical: guilt, pervasive loss of interest, great fatigue, seriously disrupted sleep, appetite and weight loss. Severely depressed, George was entered in the drug study.

Carl Davis contacted a psychiatrist approximately a year and a half after the development of a depression. His computer-repair work involved being in South America for periods of three to four months followed by periods of about the same length in the United States. The depression had developed after he had sustained a hand injury that interfered with his ability to perform his job. Despite excellent medical care, the injury was recovering so slowly that he could not work.

Prior to his injury Carl had been a hardworking and competent young man who had many friends and married early. His major psychological difficulty had stemmed from his divorce. During his work-related travels his wife had gone through law school and had begun to feel that their lives were now too different. The marriage had been unexciting but had seemed stable, and Carl was surprised when his wife asked for a divorce. They tried marriage counseling, but it did not save the marriage. A few years later Carl fell in love with another woman, whom he plans to marry.

Following the injury Carl had vivid flashbacks of the accident and noted that he was becoming increasingly anxious and depressed. He returned to school in order to retool with another degree. For the first time he found school difficult and his concentration and memory impaired. He also began to have episodes of dizziness, light-headedness, and palpitations.

In seeking help, Carl first consulted a group of nonmedical psychotherapists, who recommended hypnotherapy along with "reality therapy" and "rational emotive therapy." He was perceived as depressed, but they recommended that antidepressants not be given because of the possible negative effect on his concentration. During the next year and a half he received intermittent psychotherapy while his condition worsened. His grades at school fell, he became anxious when he left the house (agoraphobia), and his self-esteem diminished "to the vanishing point." His psychological problems were worsened by his physical ones. His injured hand could not be repaired sufficiently to allow him to return to his job. At this point he consulted the psychiatrist.

Long-Term Depression

The case described here differs from the others in the long-term nature of the illness, which had been misdiagnosed in the patient's earlier years.

Edith Forbes, a participant in a drug study with a new antidepressant medication, had been depressed for approximately ten years and had received two rounds of psychotherapy during that time. As a child and adolescent, she had had symptoms that were at first considered neurotic, the result of growing up in a difficult family.

Edith had been the oldest of four girls raised by a mother described as spoiled, demanding, and greedy, who became an alcoholic during the patient's early childhood and adolescence. The mother apparently did not feel and certainly did not express warm or loving feelings. She punished the patient with sarcasm and contempt. No help was available from Edith's father, who was a psychological absentee—he showed no interest in her.

The family lived in the country, and Edith had few friends—although those she had were close and she valued them highly. She dealt with the family situation by withdrawal and reading. A tall woman, she had gone through a particularly gawky adolescence, accurately described herself as unattractive, and did not begin to date until she entered college. Nevertheless, she made a fine marriage to a thoughtful, caring, and loving man.

Edith functioned well on a number of jobs and ran a shipshape home. Her other major interest continued to be reading, and she also played some golf. She felt that she had been programmed to achieve and on her job was very competitive and sarcastic (she was aware of the irony of being like her mother), feeling adequate only when she could degrade her peers. Unhappy at this situation, she finally entered psychotherapy.

At some time during her first psychotherapy, the quality of her mood changed. She lost interest in golf, her sex drive diminished, her irritability increased, and she began to behave unpleasantly to members of her family as well as to coworkers.

The two courses of psychotherapy, which together consumed more than three years spread out over almost a decade, convinced her that her problems were the result of her experiences, but she remained irritable and competitive, and still had few interests in life.

Mania

It is relatively easy to understand that depressed people are sick. They look miserable and often function poorly. Yet, strangely, many depressed patients at times feel excessively good. These periods are called manic episodes. Some manias occur when the patient has never been depressed. A person is considered manic if she (1) has a prolonged period during which she is euphoric, elevated, "flying"; and (2) has a number of the following symptoms: inflated self-esteem, or the feeling that she is better, wiser, superior to others; a markedly decreased need to sleep (for example, managing on a few hours a night); a tendency to monopolize conversations, talking rapidly and excessively; the feeling that her thoughts are flowing so rapidly that she cannot express them in an orderly fashion; increased activity—socially, at work or school, or sexually; impulsive behavior that often leads to trouble, such as buying sprees, promiscuity, and rash business decisions. Manic periods can be variable in duration, and frequently they are followed by severe depression, so that this combination of symptoms is commonly known as manic-depression.

It is easiest to understand the manic patient by thinking of mania as the flip side of depression. When in a manic state, the depressed patient no longer lacks interest in life but is transformed into exactly the opposite kind of person. The manic is interested in everything and is bubbling over with plans. His sense of optimism sweeps all doubts aside, and he often impulsively pursues impossible, unrealistic goals.

The depressive's lack of self-esteem is replaced by a grandiose conviction of tremendous power and superhuman capacities. The manic patient usually feels on top of the world, although some are intensely hostile and irritable and engage in furious squabbles and fights, alienating friends, business associates, and family. Many divorces occur when one partner has become manic and the other finds the change intolerable.

The manic seems to be having such a good time that it is difficult for most people to consider him ill, especially when the illness is a variation of the illness that makes people depressed. The manic patient also does not believe that he is sick and usually refuses treatment. This is enormously unfortunate because excellent medications, such as lithium, are available for manic-depression. Therefore, the family members or friends have the extra burden of talking the patient into treatment.

Aaron Baker had been an energetic, prosperous businessman. His partners began to notice that he was working much longer hours and coming up with many more ingenious and creative ideas about how to make money. Initially skeptical about some of Aaron's ideas, his partners gradually became convinced that he was an authentic business genius. He was sensationally successful at persuading others of the merits of his schemes. He was his own best salesman, showing a dazzling command of facts and figures, and unshakable confidence. However, his partners were taken aback when he told them of his plans for a half-billion-dollar chain of health resorts throughout the United States promoting a secret Russian treatment that would restore youth and sexual potency to older persons. Aaron produced detailed demographic projections to support his ideas.

Because of the enormous investment necessary, some of Aaron's partners asked for more details about the nature of the secret miracle treatment. Aaron was outraged by such questioning of his judgment, and during several very unpleasant scenes he uncharacteristically ranted and raved about their lack of support. Several of his partners gave in, but one insisted on seeing some proof that this was not some fly-by-night fad.

The partners were also somewhat disconcerted because the formerly staid, hardworking Aaron now seemed to have become a member of the jet set, with frequent flights to and from Europe in the company of attractive research assistants. His drinking had also increased substantially.

Financial and personal disaster finally struck when the partners discovered that there was no proof whatsoever of the usefulness of the new wonder treatment. Big investors refused to join the undertaking, and the company's large preliminary investment was irretrievably lost. Aaron quit the company, saying that he was surrounded by fools and assassins. His bewildered wife finally told him that perhaps he should get some help and received a storm of abuse for her well-meaning efforts.

Several months later Aaron became depressed. At first he attributed this to his loss of money, friends, and business. But eventually he became very inactive and quiet, interested in nothing and responsive to no one. He was finally hospitalized.

Treatment

Most of the patients that we have described here are victims of biological depression, although in some of them the symptoms take the form of physical ailments, unusual behavior change, or substance abuse. For almost all of them, medication was very helpful, in some instances producing improvement when other forms of treatment had not done so previously. For patients whose depression is less severe or more clearly related to life circumstances, other treatments—primarily psychotherapy—or even the passage of time might serve as well, but the point we are emphasizing in this book is that for people who are incapacitated by biological depression, treatment with medication should usually be the first choice. The excerpts that follow illustrate some of the recovery patterns that can accompany treatment of this kind.

Jill Jason

Jill Jason finally became completely inactive. She didn't eat, she didn't sleep, and she didn't talk. On her doctor's advice her husband took her to a psychiatric ward in a general hospital. The hospital staff gave her a thorough physical examination and found nothing wrong except the effects of malnutrition. Jill thought that she was being punished for her sins. Her psychiatrist prescribed an antidepressant but warned her husband that often these drugs take three to four weeks to work.

During the first week Jill slept somewhat better and began to eat a little. During the second week she occasionally responded to her husband's questions or to comments about what was happening with the family.

On the seventeenth day of her treatment, when Jill's husband walked into her room he was astonished to see her sitting by the bed reading the newspaper. She gave him a big smile and asked how the children were. Jill's husband was flabbergasted. She almost looked like her old self. Jill said that it was like a curtain had been raised and that for the first time in months she could really feel and respond.

Over the next week her progress was astounding. She was the old Jill—laughing, optimistic, and full of plans to fix up the house. Her doctor warned them that she would have to continue on the medication for at least six months and that she would need regular checkups during this period.

Mary Stenn

Mary Stenn's last boyfriend told her something must be wrong with her because she was constantly selling herself short. Further, he could not understand why somebody so attractive and intelligent wasn't getting anywhere. Mary had thought of herself as being attractive and intelligent when she was a teenager, but lately she had lost faith in herself. Finally, at the boyfriend's suggestion, she entered psychotherapy. However, after many months she hadn't improved.

Mary's therapist told her that her new low self-esteem and performance difficulties were due to fear of success. He suggested that her devoted parents had made an unconscious bargain with her: they would take care of her if only she would remain their little girl. Therefore, Mary must learn to become independent of her parents. When she had achieved independence, her depression would go away. These ideas seemed reasonable to Mary, although occasionally she thought that perhaps she was being dependent on her parents—and now on her therapist—because she was depressed, rather than the other way around.

After almost a year of therapy with no signs of change, Mary's parents told her that they would no longer pay her rent if she didn't switch from a psychotherapist to a psychiatrist. Mary discussed this with her therapist, who pointed to the possibility that again she might simply be heeding interfering parents and that perhaps she ought to give the psychotherapy more time. However, Mary was also getting somewhat discouraged with the psychotherapy since little seemed to be happening. She grudgingly agreed to a consultation with a psychiatrist.

The psychiatrist said that she thought Mary was depressed and would give her an antidepressant. She told Mary that there were several different sorts of antidepressants available and that if the first didn't work she shouldn't get discouraged. Initially the doctor prescribed the same sort of antidepressant that had been so successful with Jill Jason. However, the medication gave Mary a dry mouth and constipation and didn't seem to help at all. She felt even more lethargic, and at times her thinking seemed muddled. She complained about this to the doctor, who told her that these medications often take four to six weeks to work and that she should stick with it. The doctor saw Mary regularly during the month to try to keep her courage up. However, Mary simply did not respond; if anything, she felt worse.

Mary's psychiatrist told her that it was too bad that the drug didn't work but that there was another whole group of drugs that often did work when the first did not. These drugs were somewhat of a nuisance to use because they required a special diet, and if the diet was broken there was a chance of unpleasant or even dangerous side effects. This was bad news for Mary, who had already lost confidence in medication. Her doctor was sympathetic and reassuring. In explaining all the pros and cons of the medication, she emphasized how Mary could benefit from it and pointed out that she couldn't continue the way she was.

Reluctantly Mary agreed, went on the diet, and took the new medicine. Although the doctor said the medicine might take several weeks to work, Mary began to feel somewhat more energetic within the first week. By the second week she had gone shopping and had bought herself some new clothes for the first time in three years. She also called her old friends.

By the third week Mary told the doctor that she might even have too much pep and that she was having difficulty sleeping. After the doctor adjusted the dosage of the medication, Mary soon simply felt good and active again. However, she had to see the doctor regularly to have her condition monitored and the dosage readjusted as necessary.

After six months Mary was working, had a new boyfriend, and was developing an interest in cooking. She was often the life of the party. Mary asked her doctor how long she had to be on the medication now that she felt perfectly well. Would she relapse? The doctor said that she couldn't answer that question. People with long-standing depressive illness often had recurrences when they went off medication. The only way to find out was to try. She said that since Mary had done so well for six months and her life seemed stable and rewarding, this seemed a good time to try.

However, Mary also wanted to know whether there would be any long-term serious side effects if she stayed on the medication for another six months. The doctor said that there would be no problem about continuing the medication for that length of time, and that they could make up their minds about discontinuing medication later. Mary was concerned because she was being considered for a promotion and she didn't want the possibility of a slump to interfere with her new career.

Mary's anxiety and panic attacks had also improved markedly. She was no longer worried that she might have a heart attack, but she was still anxious about the possible return of the feelings of panic. She was afraid that if she went off the medication they might come back.

Milton Meyer

Milton Meyer began to examine every aspect of his life carefully. He attributed his apathy to a midlife crisis, which he understood was fairly common among men his age as they recognized that their adult life was half over. He had read of existential psychotherapy, which addressed such issues, and after discussing it with a close friend who was a psychologist, he entered therapy.

In the process of self-examination he began to belittle his work as a surgeon and minimize his contributions; he began to view himself as someone who had been programmed by his family and background and had lived his life according to their schedule. He saw himself as living out his parents' wishes for *themselves* in regard to his choice of career, spouse, and lifestyle. He also began to feel, first from a philosophical standpoint and later from an emotional one, that life might not be worth living and that suicide deserved serious consideration—a rational response to an irrational existence.

At this juncture Milton's psychotherapist became worried and referred Milton to a psychiatrist with whom he sometimes worked. Because many of the psychotherapeutic interpretations had made sense to Milton, the psychiatrist had difficulty in convincing him that a major depression, of biological origin, might be playing a role in the evolution of his feelings. The psychiatrist wisely did not challenge Milton's intellectual stance, recognizing that he would rather abandon psychiatric treatment than give up his painfully acquired insights. When the psychiatrist queried Milton about his symptoms, he found many that had been unreported simply because Milton had not been asked about them by the psychologist, whose treatment focus had not been on depression as a possible disease. In addition to Milton's disproportionate self-criticism, suicidal thoughts, and a loss of interest in his usual pursuits, he had noticeable sleep problems, awakening frequently in the middle of the night and early in the morning, a decrease in ability to concentrate, diminished sexual interest, and a characteristic fluctuation of his symptoms during the course of the day.

The psychiatrist finally persuaded Milton that medication might constitute a useful adjunctive treatment to help with the physiological problems (which Milton believed had come from his psychological ones) and that he should continue to work on his psychological ones in therapy. When tricyclic antidepressants were administered, Milton experienced improvement of his depression in the expected sequence. His sleep problems diminished and had disappeared by two weeks, his energy and concentration slowly improved, by six weeks he was regaining his interest in surgery, the violin, and gardening, and in successive weeks he experienced increasing affection for his family, a return of his sex drive, and a marked lessening of his philosophical concerns. The psychiatrist suggested maintaining drug treatment, citing evidence that such depressions have a natural history that must be played out, and during that time medication usually suppresses symptoms. Milton gladly agreed and began to rethink his psychotherapeutic experience.

He continued to believe that he had experienced a midlife crisis and that it had been important for him to reevaluate his life goals at that particular time. He also continued to believe that to some extent his parents' expectations had programmed him—as such expectations do for most people—but over time he considered this less important, recognizing that the only way not to program a child is to bring him up without human companionship on a desert island. When his medication was diminished and discontinued after a year and a half, Milton reexperienced a recurrent slight but identifiable loss of interest in his customary activities. He was placed on antidepressants again, and repeated attempts were made every few months to discontinue them. Five years later he still required small maintenance doses of antidepressants in order to avoid recurrence of severe depression.

Bob Rush

Bob Rush had now been to three gastroenterologists. He had had a GI series, a lower bowel series, and a barium enema. Nothing had been found. The last doctor stated firmly that continued tests were going to be a waste of time and that even if President Reagan had had a colonoscopy that didn't mean that Bob should have one.

However, the doctor had just read that antidepressants were often helpful for people with bowel complaints for which there didn't seem to be any physical cause. Bob said that he would go for anything if the doctor thought it might work.

Bob was started on medication and after several weeks his abdominal distress disappeared. He no longer felt he had to check out bathroom locations. His work improved, and he suddenly found that he was also enjoying life a great deal more. Looking back, he could see that he had been in a real slump without knowing it.

Marge Pearl

Marge Pearl had refused to go to doctors several times, and her husband was getting fed up with her growing abuse of alcohol. He finally told her that unless she got help he was going to leave. Marge replied that all her troubles were due to him but he shouldn't leave.

The Pearls agreed instead to see a marriage counselor. The counselor listened to their mutual complaints for several weeks and then told Marge that he thought she needed something more than marriage counseling because she was drunk half the time. During this period her husband's resolve to leave unless she got adequate care had been strengthened by their discussions. Marge also was becoming increasingly aware that everything was not her husband's fault and that she had an illness that was destroying their lives.

The marriage counselor recommended a psychiatrist to whom he had often referred patients. When Marge saw the psychiatrist, he told her that she was clearly abusing alcohol but that he thought she was doing this secondarily to the severe depression that she had manifested before the excessive alcohol use began. He treated her with an antidepressant, and after several weeks Marge's mood substantially improved and she found herself resorting to alcohol less. However, her mood was very variable, and she continued to have bad weeks. The doctor suggested that adding lithium to the first medication might help. When the combination was tried, Marge's mood became quite stable.

With the improvement in Marge's outlook, she and her husband were able to work together again in marriage counseling. They did have real differences about many aspects of their life together, but now they could begin to make useful compromises instead of simply giving up and heading rapidly toward divorce.

Saul Schwartz

Saul Schwartz refused to take antidepressants. He said that he wasn't depressed, that he just had a backache. He also refused to see a psychiatrist because that was for crazy people. His doctor and the family talked to him many times but accomplished nothing. Finally, at the instigation of Saul's desperate family, the family doctor took a real risk and told Saul that he had a new medicine that was good for backs. Saul was not told that it was actually an antidepressant.

Since Saul was still a free citizen who was in complete charge of his own life, this was a violation of his civil liberties. Patients should not be forced or misled into taking medication against their will. Only if they go through a legal hearing and are declared incompetent by a court can their decisions be put aside. In some states even this is not enough and the courts demand a re-review of all such medication orders even if the patient has already been found incompetent. Thus, the paternalistic actions of Saul's doctor were highly risky. Even the agreement of Saul's family that the prescription of a misidentified medication was necessary would be an inadequate defense in a lawsuit.

Saul didn't like the new medication much because it gave him a dry mouth and constipation, and he wanted to stop taking it after a few days. However, his wife carried on so that he agreed to take the new pills just to have a little peace.

In a few weeks Saul became more active and started talking about going back to work. He also started to laugh for the first time in months. When asked if he was feeling better, he said he felt just the same as he always did, and that his only problem was his back, which seemed a little less bothersome. He still didn't understand why other people had ever called him depressed. He also didn't see why his wife kept insisting that he continue his medication.

Ralph and John White

Ralph White's family was shocked to hear that their son was a drug abuser. They immediately took him to a psychotherapist, whom Ralph saw regularly twice a week for six months. During this time his grades didn't improve, and he was spending more time out late at night with questionable companions. When his parents complained to his psychotherapist, the therapist said that such direct contact between them and him was interference with therapy. Ralph had to understand that the therapist was on his side and not simply an agent of the parents.

That sounded reasonable, but the situation wasn't getting any better. Ralph's uncle told the parents that he had heard that a lot of these drug problems could be treated with medicine. Mr. and Mrs. White reacted negatively to this suggestion. After all, Ralph's problem was with drugs in the first place, so wouldn't additional drugs just complicate the problem?

After a year Ralph refused to see the psychotherapist any longer, saying that it was boring and a waste of time. The therapist said that Ralph had quit because they were getting close to the source of his difficulties. Ralph's friends told him that it was about time that he quit seeing "that shrink" because all his troubles were due to his parents' puritanical attitudes anyway. Ralph's parents oscillated between trying to ignore his difficulties, in the vain hope that he would snap out of it, and erupting into harsh shouting. Ralph continued to spend large amounts of time out with his friends. It was unclear how he was getting money for the drugs since he wasn't working.

Since at the same time John White had quit work in response to his own troubles, Mrs. White was in despair at having two emotional cripples on her hands. She suggested psychotherapy for her husband, but John said that it hadn't helped Ralph, so why should he try? However, when the family physician insisted that medication would help, John started to take antidepressants. Within a month he was no longer depressed. He slept well, ate well, had a restored interest in sex, and looked forward to getting another job. He was still desperately worried about his son, but he wasn't depressed.

Armed with the knowledge that medication had helped him, John told his son that he would have to move out if he didn't go to a psychiatrist for medication. Ralph preferred to move out, and bummed around for a year. Finally, strung out and broke, he returned home. His parents insisted that he have a psychiatric evaluation, and eventually he was treated with the same medication that had helped his father. His mood improved in six weeks, and he became interested in returning to school. He still used a great deal of pot and associated with semi-delinquent buddies. His former bright future now seemed unlikely. His parents felt that if they had caught his depression earlier, his change in lifestyle and the wasted year might have been avoided.

George Harris

When George Harris began to participate in the experimental drug study at the Depression Clinic, the psychiatrist also met with him half an hour per week for nine weeks, the duration of the study. The first fifteen minutes of each session were occupied by formal questioning and the filling out of forms. For the second fifteen minutes, during which the therapist was silent most of the time, George would reflect aloud on his condition. During this nine weeks his sense of sadness and other symptoms gradually seemed to disappear, and he began to act in a problem-solving way. After he discussed the forthcoming separation with his daughter and she elected to stay with him, he contacted a lawyer. Rather than passively resigning, he began to contest the divorce. He also investigated alternative job opportunities.

After nine weeks George was rated as moderately improved, but he had turned his life around. In the study, however, it turned out that he had been on *placebo*. George then accepted the option of taking the experimental drug. But in four weeks, before the drug had time to act, he had completely recovered.

George's story illustrates several characteristics of depression. First, some patients get better on placebo; second, many patients get better with the passage of time; third, many patients get better with the opportunity to talk things out with a therapist. George had not been receiving formal psychotherapy, but he had ventilated his feelings with the physician, who was sympathetic even though he made no suggestions or interpretations and engaged in no other standard psychotherapeutic maneuvers. The therapist listened while George came to terms with himself and began to solve his realistic problems.

Carl Davis

When the psychiatrist first saw Carl Davis, he was a downcast young man who talked slowly while recounting his symptoms and brooded about his hand injury. He had lost interest in everything but his fiancée and was extremely anxious, guilty, and preoccupied with thoughts of suicide. He was close to failing at school, because he could neither concentrate on nor remember what he was studying. He had lost fifteen pounds, had no energy or sex drive, and although he fell asleep easily, after an hour he awoke and tossed and turned for the rest of the night. His diagnosis was biological depression, triggered by life events, which had persisted for a year and a half and had been unresponsive to psychotherapy.

Carl's symptoms were classic, the kind that would be pointed out to medical students as typical of biological depression. Nevertheless, because the previous therapist had avoided a medical consultation and antidepressants, Carl may have had one and a half years of inadequate treatment and unnecessary suffering. He was begun on a tricyclic antidepressant and responded quickly. Within two weeks his sleep difficulty was gone, at four weeks his interest in school returned, and by the tenth week of antidepressant therapy he was functioning as well as he had before the accident. His grades moved from C's to A's, and he and his fiancée moved in together.

The psychiatrist expected that Carl would remain demoralized because of his permanent physical handicap, which prevented him from doing work he enjoyed very much, but he took care of his demoralization himself. Without prompting, he recounted multiple instances in his life when he had been stymied but by personal efforts had succeeded. One year later, with minimal psychotherapy, he is functioning well, and the dose of medication is being reduced to see if his depression has disappeared. He is planning to get married soon and fully enjoys life.

Edith Forbes

Ten years late, Edith Forbes recognized her symptoms in a research advertisement for depressed subjects. In the study, she was first treated with an experimental drug, which worked, and then with a standard drug, which also worked. As the depressive symptoms responded, Edith became more interested in her job, her house, her golf, and her sex life. She worried less about trivia and suddenly realized that even her mind was working better—she had not previously noticed that she had been reading less and getting less out of it. The most surprising feature of her response to the antidepressants was the gradual withering away of her neurotic symptoms. She became less concerned with one-upmanship, she no longer felt the need to be a star, she became more gregarious, and her barbed hostility disappeared.

Edith has now been receiving antidepressants for three years. When they are gradually lowered or stopped, she does not suffer a full recurrence of depression but her personality reverts to what it was like in her predepression period.

Apparently a chronic mild depression increased Edith's neurotic response to her disturbing family. An awareness of the origin of some of her personality traits did not help her, but medical relief from the depression seems to have allowed her to change and grow in ways she could not before. In an autobiographical account she describes herself as now "knowing where I want to direct my life . . . I am much kinder now . . . I no longer rely on degrading peers. I now like myself and am very secure in who I am. . . . I believe that this attitude has resulted from my growing in wisdom and maturity. . . . My family agrees wholeheartedly and enjoys living with me."

Aaron Baker

Aaron Baker responded very well to the antidepressants that were given to him in the hospital. His ability to experience pleasure returned and he began to show interest in his former activities. However, he told his wife and doctor that he had a brilliant idea that would bring back his lost fortune. He refused to believe that he had been sick before his depression. He viewed his mania as simply the way he was when he was normal. Finally, to placate his wife, he accepted the psychiatrist's suggestion that he go on lithium. His mood now shifted to normal. He was able to realize that his grandiose goals were indeed unrealistic and that his feelings of constant exhilaration had themselves been symptoms of an illness.

Understanding Depression

With these examples of the kinds of problems that depressed people can have, and of the good responses that many depressed patients have to medication, we hope we have conveyed some sense of the nature of the illness. In the rest of the book we shall go into more detail about the course of depression; theories about its causes; diagnosis and treatment; and ways to get help.

CHAPTER

3 The Course of Depression: What Happens to Depression Over Time?

The Onset of Depression

WHEN DO THE various forms of depression usually begin? Physicians used to believe that such disorders began in middle age. As we have become more expert at diagnosing these illnesses, we have found that they often begin much earlier. Until the past ten years psychiatrists believed that depression was extremely uncommon in adolescents and children. However, with increasing evidence that depression is inherited, psychiatric researchers have begun to study the children of parents with these disorders and have found that clear-cut symptoms of depression—usually mild—can often be identified in such children. Frequently these depressions in children are unknown to the parents and are found only when the children are interviewed. Similarly, depression is now recognized as quite common in adolescents.

A medical description of the course or "natural history" of an illness indicates its possible outcomes: how long it lasts, what proportion of the patients get better or worse, and how quickly patients recover without treatment. The natural history of depression follows several common patterns, and in most of them the symptoms will likely return from time to time. However, those symptoms can usually be controlled. In the following sections we will discuss the course of depressive illness and then will add a description of the course of manic-depression, which is even more variable.

Alternate Patterns of Depressive Illness

Well ——→ depressive illness ——→ well

In the form *Well——depressive illness——well*, a person is going along without any life problems—minding his own business, so to speak. Then, either in reaction to life difficulties or for no apparent reason, he becomes depressed.

These depressions usually last from about six months to two years. The number of such depressive episodes that a person experiences varies tremendously. Some people have only one attack of illness, some people have several, and an unfortunate few suffer many attacks. The intervals between attacks also vary considerably. Sometimes episodes occur in bunches and do not recur for many years, while in other instances depressive episodes occur at widely spaced intervals.

Well ——→ depressive illness ——→ treatment ——→ well ——→
treatment discontinuation ——→ mild chronic depression

In this pattern a person who develops a depressive illness is treated with medication; after several weeks or months, the patient feels better and the medication is diminished and then stopped. The person no longer experiences the symptoms of intense depressive illness, which was treated, but he or she does not feel up to par. For example, the patient's interest in his usual activities may not have completely returned, and he may still be rather passive, with decreased self-esteem and decreased energy. These are the symptoms of mild depressive illness.

These mild symptoms can be eliminated by the same medication that treated the severe depressive illness, but their control requires the continuing administration of the medication. In other words, the patient must continue to receive antidepressant medication regularly if he or she is not to suffer a relapse into mild depressive illness symptoms.

Mild chronic depression ⟶ depressive illness ⟶ treatment ⟶ well ⟶ treatment discontinuation ⟶ mild chronic depression

In this pattern the patient has been mildly and chronically depressed from adolescence or even childhood, develops a depressive illness that is treated, and experiences well-being. When his medication is discontinued, he then returns to his state of mild depression. Interestingly, before they have the depressive illness, many of these patients do not know they had always been depressed. But when the patient develops depressive illness and is successfully treated with medication, he feels better than he has ever felt in his life. This is not because medication has made him high or manic. It is simply that when the symptoms are removed, the patient notices the difference. Such a patient is similar to a child with a vision defect who begins to wear glasses that successfully compensate for the defect. When such a child realizes that he now has no difficulty in figuring out what is on the blackboard, he begins to see himself differently. To be exact, we cannot say that a depressed patient of this kind has been depressed since birth, but we can often say that he or she has been depressed as far back as he or she can remember; in many instances this may be as early as five or six years of age.

Well ⟶ mild depression ⟶ well ⟶ mild depression, etc.

Not only severe depressive illness but also mild depression can occur in episodes. When mild depressions appear and disappear on an irregular basis, they are often not noticed or are mistaken for psychological depressions. As we mentioned in Chapter 2, it is not severity that distinguishes a biological depressive illness from a nonbiological depression but the pattern of symptoms. The same persons who experience severe episodes of depressive illness may at other times experience similar but less intense episodes of depression. Recognition of the nature of their illness is important because they frequently respond to medication and may not to psychotherapy. Certainly if psychotherapy has not been effective within three months, medication should be considered.

Manic-Depression

The course of manic-depression can be much more varied than the course of depressive illness, because any new episode can be either up (the manic phase of the illness) or down (the depressive phase). In addition, both up episodes and down ones can be either mild or severe.

How often new episodes occur varies a great deal, from only one attack of manic illness in a lifetime to several per year. Lithium, the major medication for manic-depression, can prevent attacks of mania or depression, it can diminish the severity of attacks, and when given for a long time, it can diminish the frequency of attacks.

Mild Manic-Depression

Some people have a manic-depressive illness in which they experience only mild forms of both symptom extremes. When they alternate in a fairly rhythmic and continuing way, they are diagnosed as "cyclothymic personality."

Ups and downs may follow one another without interruption, or they may be separated by normal intervals that can last for months. Such people are often referred to as moody. Once one knows what to look for, the regular alternation of mood in this disorder makes it fairly easy to recognize.

Recurrence of Depression

Patients frequently ask this important question: "If I have had one attack of depression, can I expect to have more?" As indicated above, the answer is "Yes." A person who has had an attack of biological depression is much more likely to have another attack than a person who has never had one. Unfortunately, we do not know the odds of recurrence for any one person, and we do not know when recurrence is likely. Sometimes attacks occur regularly every spring or fall, sometimes they appear in bunches, sometimes they appear years apart, and sometimes a person suffers a depressive episode and then never has another one.

Manic-depression is much more likely than other forms of depression to recur frequently. Because of its great risk of recurrence, manic-depressive patients are often given lithium as preventive treatment. We will discuss lithium further in the chapter on treatment. Studies organized by the National Institute of Mental Health have found that the average person with manic-depressive disorder "loses" nine years from his or her life. That is, the person is unable to function as a student, homemaker, or worker for a total of nine years (usually spread out over a number of episodes). *Without treatment*, the average person with manic-depressive illness is "out of commission" for nine of the forty-nine years between twenty-one and seventy, or about eighteen percent of his or her adult life. This does not include the frequent troubles manic-depressive patients have in their marriages, or the difficulties they have in other areas. At least half of manic patients have serious marital problems. Many manic-depressives with manic symptoms drink to the point of alcoholism.

Suicide

The most tragic outcome in depressive illness and manic-depression is suicide. Suicide occurs in ten to fifteen percent of untreated or *inadequately* treated depressive and manic-depressive illnesses. Depressive illness is a leading cause of death (the second most common cause among adolescents and the eighth in adults). Because depressive illness is easily recognizable and usually easily treatable, many of the deaths that result from the disease must be seen as unnecessary. One of the aims of this book is to lessen the extent of this great social tragedy by helping more people suffering from depressive illness to secure proper help.

CHAPTER
4 What Causes Depression?

THE MAJORITY of cases of depressive illness appear to be *genetically transmitted* and *chemically produced*. Stated differently, the disorder seems to be hereditary, and what is inherited is a tendency to chemical imbalance in the *brain*. Antidepressant medications apparently have a compensatory effect on the imbalance that is believed to cause depressive illness.

Patterns of Depressive Illness in Families

Although depressive illness does occur at a higher rate in particular families, it does not always "breed true" and sometimes can skip generations. A grandparent may have the disorder, but his or her children may escape, or may have related problems with alcohol; subsequently the grandchildren may show symptoms of the illness. The type of depressive illness can also vary from one generation to another. It is not uncommon for a parent to be manic-depressive and for the child to have a depressive illness without the manic aspect. Finally, heredity does not seem to be an all-or-none matter. Close relatives may inherit either severe forms or mild forms of depressive illness or manic-depression.

Heredity Versus Environment

The tendency of depressive illness to run in families has been recognized for hundreds of years. Nevertheless, until recently there was no positive way of determining whether this was the result of heredity or environment. Certainly the degree to which depressive illness and manic-depression are manifested in both parents and children does not tell us whether nature or nurture is more important. Some learned traits run overpoweringly in families—for example, with few exceptions the children of English-speaking parents speak English. On the other hand, some genetic traits appear in families inconsistently—for example, not all of the children of a redheaded parent have red hair.

The problem of distinguishing between effects of nature and nurture seemed insoluble until investigators in the 1960s hit upon the straightforward and simple technique of studying adopted persons. In adoptees one set of parents supplies the genes, while the other supplies the environment. If a psychiatric illness is psychologically caught from a psychologically disturbed parent, early removal from that parent should prevent the later development of the disorder. But if the disorder is genetically passed from parent to child, the adult adoptee has just as great a risk of developing the illness in question as he would have had if he had not been removed from his biological parents. The adoption strategy has been applied to the study of several psychiatric illnesses, including depressive illness and manic-depression.

These studies have found that heredity plays a role in depressive illness and manic-depression. They have not found any evidence that severe forms of these illnesses are produced psychologically by depression or mania in the adoptive parents. The studies have also found that suicide—

the most serious consequence of depressive illness—has powerful genetic contributions. In one comparison between adopted persons who developed depressive illness and adopted persons who did not develop such illness it was found that suicide was eleven times as great among the biological relatives of adopted depressives as it was in the biological relatives of adopted nondepressives.

In early 1987 the National Institute of Mental Health announced that researchers had located a gene that triggers a variety of manic-depression, dramatically confirming the hypothesis that had emerged from the adoption studies and other evidence. As science writer Philip J. Hilts wrote in the *Washington Post*, the discovery established "biological proof of the theory that [manic-depression] is an inheritable, genetically based disease."

Genes Plus Events Can Equal Depression

Many people have misconceptions about genetic illnesses. Even if an illness is genetic, that does *not* mean that other factors do not also play a role in its development. For some people depressive illness appears for no apparent reason and disappears as if it is following its own internal schedule. In others, life experience seems to trigger a depressive illness. Some people have a seasonal depressive illness, apparently related to a decrease in the length of the day, which occurs in the fall and lasts until the spring. Many of these people might be "cured" if they moved closer to the equator, where the amount of daylight remains about the same throughout the year. Seasonal depressions clearly show a mixture of hereditary and environmental effects; many of us may become somewhat down during the darker months of the year, but few of us develop depressive illness.

Still other individuals appear to develop a severe depressive illness following the loss of a loved one or a major disappointment. Such persons show a decreased psychological resilience, an inability to cope with stresses that most people can overcome. This vulnerability is very similar to that in a number of medical illnesses in which individuals inherit a chemical abnormality that may cause problems only when they are exposed to a particular environment. As an example, many Mediterranean people inherit a tendency to develop anemia but never show symptoms of that disease unless they eat broad beans or go to the Far East and take a particular antimalarial drug. Their disorder is genetic but is triggered by life events.

Can Upbringing Cause Depressive Illness?

Since Sigmund Freud began to theorize early in the twentieth century on the origins of mental illness, some of his ideas have been elaborated into the popular notion that various psychological experiences can produce a tendency to develop a depressive illness in later life. However, unlike the situation with the genetic theories, little solid scientific information exists to support theories relating early experiences to later depression. Even these theories acknowledge that most people exposed to difficult early life experiences (for example, loss of both parents in early life, frequent changes in caretakers, gross neglect, etc.) do not develop depressive illness in later life. The fact that only a fraction of such people do become seriously depressed raises the obvious question of whether these individuals were genetically predisposed to develop depressive illness. Nevertheless, it is possible that some genetically predisposed depressions would not occur without precipitating early trauma. This remains speculative.

Chemistry and Depression

The information that supports the view that depressive illness results from a chemical imbalance comes from studies of both people and animals. Human studies have shown that seriously depressed persons may differ from normal persons (1) in brain electrical activity, both awake and sleeping; (2) in brain chemicals thought to play a major role in the regulation of emotion; and (3) in the chemistry of certain types of blood cells. A few studies that have been made of the brains of depressed individuals who have committed suicide indicate that there are some chemical differences between these brains and those of nondepressed persons. Investigators are also beginning to learn a great deal from new technical instruments such as the PET scan, both about brain activity in persons with illnesses of this kind and about brain changes induced by medication.

Additional information comes from the study of the effects of antidepressant medication in humans and in animals. For example, people with depressive illness who are given such medication usually get better; people without depression who are given antidepressant medication may develop unpleasant side effects but they show no elevation in mood. It is assumed that these different reactions can be explained by differences in the brain chemistry of people with and without depressive illness.

Supportive evidence also comes from direct examination of the tissues and brains of animals who have been administered antidepressant medication. The observable changes in animal brain chemistry in response to these drugs have generated theories about drug functioning in humans that are being tested clinically. Causal questions are far from answered, but with such powerful investigative techniques, explanatory facts are gradually falling into place like pieces in a jigsaw puzzle.

During the past thirty years there has been an explosion in knowledge about the structure and functioning of the brain. One major discovery has been that nerve impulses are transmitted chemically in the brain. In brain activity, neurones (cells) release minute amounts of specific chemicals—neurotransmitters—that reach other cells and cause them to react in various ways. There are many kinds of brain chemicals, and the different portions of the brain use different ones. Drugs that affect depressive illness and manic-depression—antidepressants and lithium—either increase or decrease the effect of brain chemicals, thus elevating or depressing mood. The drugs seem to act in several ways, and people with depressive illness apparently differ from one another and from people without depressive illness in terms of their particular response to medication. For example, the drugs can prevent important neurotransmitters from being absorbed or broken down by other brain cell action, or they can make neurones more sensitive to smaller amounts of such neurotransmitters.

These drugs have also been studied in humans indirectly by measurement of the excretion of brain-related chemicals in the urine or in the spinal fluid bathing the brain. Circumstantial evidence suggests that different chemical errors may produce the same or very similar symptoms. For this reason patients differ with respect to the drug or combination of drugs that may be best for them.

Illnesses That Don't Cause Depression

Two disorders that are sometimes thought to produce depression *rarely*, if ever, do so. The first is hypoglycemia. Hypoglycemia, an uncommon disorder, refers to a drop in the amount of sugar in the blood to an abnormal level. When this occurs, the body tries to compensate—for example, by releasing adrenalin, which raises blood sugar and produces sweating, muscle tension, rapid heartbeat, and anxiety. There are distinct diseases associated with hypoglycemia, but they occur infrequently. The misdiagnosis of hypoglycemia as the culprit responsible for other diseases (such as depression) is now common; hypoglycemia is hardly ever the cause of depressive illness.

The second supposed cause of depression is an allergic reaction to food or to *common* environmental chemicals. There is no evidence that serious depressive illness is ever produced by such allergies. Considerable time and money are sometimes wasted pursuing these medical will-o'-the wisps.

Predicting Depressive Illness

At the same time that medical researchers have learned more about the genetic origin of depressive illnesses, they have recognized that the evidence points to an increased likelihood of the appearance of depression in particular families. The chances that any one child will develop depression cannot be estimated exactly, but it has been predicted, for example, that thirty percent of the daughters of mothers with depressive illness will develop depressive illness themselves. This is obviously distressing, but an awareness of a genetic tendency helps a concerned parent or the vulnerable individual to detect the illness when it is beginning to develop. Early detection can mean early appropriate treatment. The depressed child, adolescent, or young adult may be spared unnecessary pain and the sometimes cumulative and far-reaching difficulties that stem from depressive illness.

We want to repeat that depressive illness and manic-depression do not necessarily breed true: parents with one form of the disorder may have offspring with another. Depressive illness may skip generations. Both mild and moderate forms of depressive illness can be genetically transmitted, and the milder forms, because of their decreased severity, are frequently misdiagnosed as psychological in origin and incorrectly treated.

Remember, if there is depressive illness or manic-depression in the family, and if a close relative becomes depressed, or if he or she develops *any* severe or unexplained psychological symptoms (for example, anxiety attacks, withdrawal, or drug abuse), it is wisest and safest to assume that he or she may have a depressive illness and to obtain a psychiatric evaluation. Depression in pre-adolescents and adolescents may have different symptoms from those seen in adults—for example, behavior problems of various kinds. Therefore any long-lasting psychological symptoms deserve careful evaluation.

5 Diagnosis and Treatment of Depression

Diagnosis

ONE OF THE major points of this book is that accurate diagnosis is necessary prior to treatment of depression. Accurate diagnosis requires both a general medical and a specialized psychiatric examination. Although most patients with depression do not have another underlying medical condition, the possibility is great enough so that an initial evaluation must include appropriate medical screening. The physical examination should include the usual blood, urine, and other laboratory tests for the most frequent abnormalities associated with depression—such as underactivity of the thyroid gland—and the physician should also be aware of rare conditions associated with depression, such as hepatitis. If the doctor suspects that one of these less common medical conditions may underlie the depression, further medical examination is indicated.

Some medications may cause depressive illness. Chief offenders are drugs used to treat high blood pressure. Though usually not the cause of the depression, they can be. Often the only way to find out is to discontinue the medications in question. This will require consultation between the psychiatrist and the physician treating the medical condition (some general physicians can do psychiatric evaluations, but most require a psychiatric consultation).

It is good practice for patients with mild depressions as well as those with severe depressions to receive a medical evaluation. There is no simple relationship between severity and the determination of whether or not a depression is biological. Most severe depressions are biological, but people who are undergoing great personal stress (grief, rejection, loss, etc.) may have severe symptoms; on the other hand, some mild chronic depressions—which may seem to be produced by life events—are associated with widespread loss of interest and pleasure (anhedonia) and are primarily biological in origin.

In the psychiatric part of the evaluation, the psychiatrist will inquire about definite signs and symptoms characteristic of depression and other psychiatric conditions. ("Symptoms" are what the patient complains about. "Signs" are what someone else may observe, such as weight loss or trembling.) Like the internist, the psychiatrist inquires about both the presence and absence of symptoms. For example, the presence of apathy indicates depression, and the absence of delusions and hallucinations helps to rule out psychosis. The diagnostician will also be interested in the patient's life and problems prior to the present depression, and in the effects of previous treatments.

Because depressive illnesses often run in families, the psychiatrist will want to know about the pattern of psychiatric illness within the patient's family. A relative's illness may provide a clue to the diagnosis of a patient whose current illness is unclear.

The process of sorting out symptoms, signs, and history to reach a diagnosis, a procedure called differential diagnosis, is essential for proper care. Effective treatments for one kind of depression may be ineffective for another and possibly even harmful for a third.

The first major question for the diagnostician is whether the patient has a biochemical depression or a psychological one. Answering this question requires great skill. Biological depression can be mild and respond to medication, while psychologically caused depression may be more severe and respond better to psychological therapy. If the diagnosis is biological depression, the diagnostician can often recognize particular types that respond better to one type of antidepressant medication than to another.

The psychiatrists who are best qualified to make this diagnosis have been well trained in modern biological psychiatry. Many nonpsychiatrist physicians, such as internists and family practitioners, diagnose and treat depression, but unfortunately many have not had the training necessary to distinguish between biological and psychological depressions. Indeed, this is still true of some psychiatrists. Similarly, many well-trained psychologists and social workers are skilled in the treatment of psychologically produced depressions but have not been taught to distinguish between biological and psychological depressions. One's best chance of getting an accurate diagnosis, therefore, will be from a psychiatrist well trained in the new biological psychiatry, sometimes called a psychopharmacologist.

After thorough diagnosis the psychiatrist can make predictions about the usefulness of pharmacological (drug) treatment, psychological treatment, or the combination of the two.

The Decision to Use Drugs, Psychotherapy, or Both: Relative Costs and Benefits

By his initial evaluation the psychiatrist can predict the likelihood of a given patient's responding to particular medications. As in the rest of medicine, perfect certainty is not possible.

Most mild depression is self-limiting, that is, it goes away by itself, without treatment, so that medication for mild depression is not always wise. However, mild depression should be followed professionally to be sure that they do not get worse. An investigation carried on at three psychiatric centers by the National Institute of Mental Health showed that for mild depression neither psychotherapy nor medication was markedly effective. However, for moderate to severe depression, medication was clearly superior, both in rapidity of effect and in the degree of benefit.

Once the patient is in treatment, the response provides a clue to diagnostic accuracy. If a long-standing condition improves after taking drugs, that tends to confirm both diagnosis and medication benefits. However, there is some trial and error in drug prescription. Patients may respond to the second or third medication prescribed rather than the first.

Even failure to respond to all known biological treatments does not necessarily mean that the patient's problems are strictly psychological. It may simply mean that useful biological treatments have not yet been developed for his particular illness.

Similarly, failure to respond to psychotherapy does not necessarily mean that one's problems are biological, since the failure may stem from inability to change entrenched ways, or possibly from a mismatch between patient and treatment (or patient and therapist).

Should drug treatment or psychotherapy be tried first? That sort of question has often been discussed in "game theory"; it involves what is called the "payoff matrix," which evaluates the advantages and disadvantages of four possibilities:

1. The patient is treated only with drugs. His depression turns out to be biological, so this is the right treatment.

2. The patient is treated only with psychotherapy. His depression turns out to be biological, so he may waste considerable time and money.
3. The patient is treated only with drugs. His depression turns out to be psychological, so the treatment is incorrect. However, that will be determined cheaply and fairly rapidly (usually within about two months; if new drug trials are required, they rarely extend as long as six months).
4. The patient is treated only with psychotherapy. His depression turns out to be psychological, so the treatment is appropriate.

Another major question concerns patients in category 3, who do not have a biological depression but receive drug treatment. All drugs produce side effects—rarely, severe ones. The risk of the major psychiatric drugs, used in therapeutic amounts with the recommended precautions, is low, probably much lower than the risk of taking penicillin or of having general anesthesia in routine surgery.

The psychiatrist can discuss the pros and cons with the patient, whose wishes should be the last word. If a doctor believes the patient's choice is unwise, then he should arrange a referral. Second opinions are also very useful for patients who find the doctor's recommendations difficult to accept.

Many physicians prefer to combine psychotherapy and medication. They believe the medication will relieve the symptoms, while the psychotherapy will enhance effective social relationships. In many instances medicine makes people accessible to psychotherapy. With the restoration of energy and zest for life, biologically depressed patients are far better equipped to deal with their internal or life problems effectively.

To us, it seems reasonable to start with medication, since it is cheaper and faster. In addition, as yet there are no data showing that psychotherapy decreases the chances of having a relapse. There are data indicating that with maintenance medication, the chances of a relapse are decreased.

We conclude that psychotherapy should not be used as a primary *treatment* of depressive illness. Unfortunately, many patients with depressive illness are often mistakenly diagnosed, both by psychiatrists and nonpsychiatrists, as having a depression caused by psychological problems and are treated with psychotherapy alone. When the depression fails to respond, many of these therapists then refer the patients to biological psychiatrists for "adjunctive" medication or "medication support." This is backwards treatment. Inappropriate psychotherapy not only can delay removal of the symptoms (with consequent bad effects on the patient's personal, vocational, and social life) but also can demoralize the patient when it fails to produce the anticipated improvement. Because psychotherapy usually provides a plausible explanation for the depression, the continuation of the symptoms leaves the patient with a sense of inadequacy and hopelessness.

Medication should be the primary treatment of depressive illness. Psychotherapy often serves only to maintain the patient's morale until medication can work. When psychotherapists refer patients for what they term "supportive" medication, a further problem sometimes arises because of conflict over which of the therapists should be in charge of treatment. We believe that the administrator of medication should have precedence, first because of the necessity of explaining to the patient the likely origin of his illness. The patient who has been receiving psychotherapy usually has to go through a process of unlearning about his depression. The psychotherapist may have been emphasizing factors that are less relevant or even inaccurate. For example, the psychotherapist may have been focusing on lengthy exploration of the patient's childhood, which in most instances—contrary to popular notions—has nothing to do with severe depressions. For some patients psychotherapy may benefit their deranged physiology, but this is still speculation.

To repeat, we think that rather than embarking on the relatively long process of psychotherapy, the patient should immediately try medication treatment. When maximally effective, such treatment consists of thorough consultations for a few weeks, followed by less frequent, brief follow-up visits.

The Effectiveness of Physical Treatment of Depression

Biological treatments for depression are dramatically effective. Over eighty percent of major depressions will respond to one or another of the antidepressant drugs, singly or in combination. Of the twenty percent of individuals with major depression who do not improve when given medication, many will then respond to electroconvulsive therapy.

Drug Treatment

Many patients have had experience with tranquilizers (such as Valium or Librium), sedatives (such as the barbiturates, Dalmane, etc.), or pep pills (such as the amphetamines). The medications used in the treatment of the biological depressions have characteristics very different from these more common psychoactive drugs.

1. Antidepressant drugs have little appreciable effect on normal mood. When taken by normal persons,

they may produce slight mental slowing rather than a high or a kick.

2. Antidepressant drugs are normalizing in contrast to other drugs affecting mood. For example, amphetamines are stimulants, producing a feeling of increased wakefulness, energy, and intellectual activity. If taken by tired, sleepy people, amphetamines temporarily produce a state of normal arousal, and if given to people who are normally awake and alert, they make them hyper. In other words, amphetamines energize regardless of where the individual starts.

   At the other extreme, sedatives decrease tension whatever the starting point: if given to overly excited persons, they tend to calm them down, while if given to people who are neither tired nor excited, they may put them to sleep.

   In describing the major antidepressant drugs as normalizing, we mean that they often make a depressed person lose his depressed feelings, but they do not have an effect on the normal person. In this respect they are similar to aspirin. Aspirin lowers a fever but of course does not lower a normal body temperature. Aspirin normalizes temperature—it does not lower normal temperature.

3. The major antidepressant drugs—tricyclic antidepressants, monoamine oxidase inhibitors, and lithium— do not attract abusive use because they do not produce high, elated feelings in normal people, although they can precipitate mania in depressed patients. As we have said earlier, they have been available for more than thirty years and have never been sold on the street.

4. Most patients with depression can stop taking the medication and remain nondepressed. Patients who

do need to continue taking antidepressants do so because their disease continues, not because the medicine has produced dependence. A depressive who continues to need medication is dependent on it in the same way that a person with high blood pressure is dependent on medication: he must control the symptoms of a continuing underlying illness. If the symptoms disappear, the medication can be stopped.

5. When antidepressants are effective, patients usually continue to derive benefit from them and do not become tolerant to their effects. This also differs from the situation with abusable drugs.

6. Unlike minor tranquilizers and stimulants, which produce benefits within an hour, these drugs do not work immediately. The effects of antidepressants rarely begin before two to four weeks and often require six weeks to reach their maximum. Further, all the benefits do not occur together. Insomnia may respond in a week and appetite may come back in two weeks, but such symptoms as lack of interest and motivation take longer to respond. The intention of treatment is to remove all the signs and symptoms.

   During treatment, the dosage required may occasionally fluctuate. If some symptoms recur—such as early morning awakening—that is a sign that the dose should be increased before other symptoms reappear.

   Many patients grow discouraged and think a drug has failed because they do not realize it has not been used long enough to work.

7. Side effects often begin when medication is started, before the positive effects begin. They usually decrease with time, but early in treatment the patient

may feel that medication is only making him feel worse.

8. The symptoms of depression may be similar from one person to another, but the presumed chemical abnormalities may differ. Unfortunately, no laboratory or chemical tests can as yet predict which drug will be best for a particular individual. A physician may have to try several different drugs before he finds the one that is most effective. Understandably, patients become concerned when this occurs, but it is a situation familiar in other branches of medicine. A good example is high blood pressure. In most instances its chemical causes—like those of depression—are not well understood. Different patients with elevated blood pressure may respond very differently to the same drugs. As with depression, the treating physician often must try several before he obtains the most effective one.

   Sometimes a drug is effective but the patient finds the side effects annoying. The most common side effects are dry mouth, constipation, light-headedness when standing, increased appetite and weight gain. The physician and patient may want to try different medications in the hope of getting equal benefits with fewer side effects.

9. At times various drugs must be combined. This procedure is also similar to the treatment of hypertension, which may require several medications. The use of more than one medicine at a time requires greater clinical skill.

10. The most effective dose—the optimal dose—varies considerably. In extreme instances, some patients may require thirty times the dose required by others. Some patients fail to respond because they have been given only a standard dose, since the treating

physician does not realize how much dosage requirements differ. Many patients who have received too little medication for their particular needs incorrectly conclude that the drug is of no use to them.

One of the major problems with treatment by family physicians is that even if they have diagnosed properly and given the right drug, they tend to be too cautious and to administer too low a dose. Therefore, patients often tell psychiatrists that they have been treated with antidepressants that have failed, whereas actually the medications have not been given a fair trial. Although the most common difficulty is too low a dose, another treatment problem is that the medications are not given for a long enough period. Antidepressants cannot be evaluated in less than four to six weeks.

11. Antidepressant medications do not affect the natural history—the lifespan—of the depressive illness. They control the symptoms while nature is taking its healing course. In this respect they are similar to aspirin, which, for example, controls the fever of flu or the pain of headache but does not shorten any illness that may be present. If antidepressants are stopped too soon, the patient may relapse. In order to prevent this, most psychiatrists wait six months after a depression has responded before they gradually reduce the dose. If depressive illness is still present, symptoms recur, but an increase in dosage will bring them under control rapidly. If symptoms do not reappear when the drug dosage is reduced, the episode of depression has probably run its course and the medication can be discontinued.

Patients who have ever had an abrupt onset to their illness often need only about six months of medication and then can discontinue without immediate relapse, although they may have another depressive episode in the future. Unfortunately, twenty to twenty-five percent of patients continue to have a mild chronic depression and may require medication for longer periods. Antidepressants have been studied carefully for almost thirty years in the treatment of large numbers of patients. Bad effects from long-term treatment have never been described. Further, these medications do not produce severe withdrawal problems on discontinuation. It is always advisable to discontinue any drug slowly. However, if these drugs are discontinued too abruptly, the worst that happens is that patients temporarily have flu-like symptoms.

12. Even though the medication may have to be taken for a long time and the illness may return if the medication is discontinued, one should not conclude that the medication is not very helpful. Most chronic diseases, such as heart disease, diabetes, and arthritis require continued use of medication for the preservation of good health. The availability of long-term medication for the chronic depressive is a step forward in the treatment of another debilitating illness.

One drug requires special mention—lithium. Lithium is the soluble form—the salt—of a metal and is very similar to sodium, its close chemical relative. Lithium's special use is in the treatment of manic-depressive illness. It can in many cases reduce or eliminate the symptoms of mania and of associated attacks of depression. When lithium is given, the dose must be carefully regulated so that concentration within the blood is kept within certain limits. Adequate intake of ordinary table salt is also necessary while taking lithium. When the dose is adequately regulated, the patient often experiences no or few side effects. Lithium is frequently given on a long-term basis—that is, for several years at a time—as a preventative drug. Its continuous use can reduce the number of episodes of recurrent manic or depressive illness that the manic-depressive patient suffers.

In any medical treatment the patient must feel comfortable with her doctor, and this is especially important in the treatment of biological depression. The doctor and patient must develop sufficient rapport so that the patient feels free to discuss all of her medical and psychological concerns. Otherwise such factors as side effects or unexpected complications in the patient's personal life might keep her from following the instructions for taking the antidepressant drugs and thus seriously limit their effectiveness. Whether the treating physician is a general practitioner, psychiatrist, or psychopharmacologist, if the patient is dissatisfied with the relationship, she should seek another doctor.

Electroconvulsive Therapy (ECT)

One of the most effective treatments for depressive illness is electroconvulsive therapy. Most of the severely ill patients who fail to respond to medication respond to ECT. Such patients are often serious risks for suicide. Recently there has been considerable concern about the use of ECT because of such past side effects as broken bones and memory loss. The idea has also been voiced that ECT is a punishment used to control unpopular behavior. To a great extent, those ideas result from earlier misuse of ECT (analogous to misuse of digitalis for "heart failure," a life-saving but dangerous drug) and lack of awareness of improvements in the technique.

The failure to recognize that ECT is a medical measure for the reversal of serious, often life-threatening illness also goes hand in hand with the belief that peculiar behavior is really a sane response to an insane political and social system. According to this belief, there is no such disease as mental illness, all treatment of mental illness is only some form of psychological or behavioral control, and ECT is a particularly punishing form of such control (the book and film *One Flew over the Cuckoo's Nest* presented this point of view). As we are emphasizing, however, the evidence is now overwhelming that there are indeed biological diseases that produce the disturbed behavior known as mental illness, and these diseases often require physical treatment. No one knows exactly how ECT works, just as no one knows exactly how digitalis works in heart disease or Dilantin in seizure disorders, but for suicidal depressive patients who have not responded to medication it is an essential treatment alternative.

Most of the serious side effects associated with ECT have been eliminated by modern techniques. When electroconvulsive treatment was first introduced, patients received neither anesthesia nor muscular relaxants and were conscious until the seizure rendered them unconscious. Lying on the bed, awaiting the shock, was very anxiety-provoking, and patients became increasingly upset with successive treatments. In some instances the force of the convulsion was very strong and the muscular contractions produced broken bones. Following the treatment, some patients reported substantial memory loss.

The modern procedure, which has largely eliminated these concerns, involves the administration of a general anesthetic and a short-acting muscular relaxant. When the therapeutic electrical impulse is delivered to the brain, the patient feels nothing and his body does not convulse. Approximately two minutes after the administration of the anesthetic, the patient awakens. He is generally somewhat confused, because of both a barbiturate hangover and the treatment itself. He is likely to remain tired and to feel somewhat fuzzy for the remainder of the day. When he has been treated as an outpatient, which is a frequent practice, someone must drive the patient home.

ECT is usually given three times per week. More frequent administrations do not seem to increase the rate of recovery. The total number of treatments required varies considerably but usually is between six and twelve—that is, the total duration of treatment is two to four weeks. Following the completion of the course of therapy, many patients have some memory deficits for the period before ECT was begun. These memory deficits tend to disappear with time, and in most instances patients suffer little chronic memory loss. Measuring the extent of the memory loss is complicated because depression itself impairs concentration and memory; the memory deficits of which the patient complains may be the product not of the ECT but of the preexisting depression. Recent changes in the placement of electrodes (unilateral) have also decreased the amount of memory loss.

The major problems still remaining in the administration of ECT arise from the use of a general anesthetic (which always involves some risk) and from the small possibility of permanent noticeable memory loss. In a person who is healthy except for severe depression, the risk of a fatal reaction to the anesthesia is minimal. The risk of memory loss affects people in different ways. A legal scholar, for example, might be handicapped by such a loss, but for many people it would be only a minor nuisance. In judging whether ECT is advisable for a particular patient, one must above all weigh against these risks the threat of suicide (again, depression has a ten to fifteen percent suicide mortality rate), but the presence of gross impairments, such as inability to eat and prolonged social and vocational withdrawal, can also affect the decision.

The Family's Role in
the Treatment of Depression

In counseling families on how to help a depressed relative, we try to make several points. First, the depressive's feelings are often completely unrelated to what is happening in his life. The depressive's business, marriage, and children may be flourishing, and yet he will feel that life is empty and barren. It is pointless to say to the depressive, "Look at all you have to live for." His feelings are irrational and he cannot be argued out of them. When he says, "I'm no good. . . . My life has been a failure. . . . Things will not get better," telling him that he's mistaken is not useful and may be demoralizing. Notice that we are not saying that the family members should agree with the patient, but merely that they shouldn't try to talk him out of those feelings, since he experiences such talk as another put-down. It *is* useful for family members to tell the patient that they are sorry that he feels so bad but that these feelings are a part of the depressive illness and will eventually diminish. The family's job is to maintain optimism and perspective.

The most serious symptom the family must recognize in a depressed person is suicidal thinking. When a depressive illness has become severe, skilled professional help is necessary immediately. The depressed person often—but not always—expresses the suicidal feelings he experiences, saying, for example, "Life is not worth living," "I'd be better off dead," "Life seems purposeless."*When family members are in doubt, they should seek a psychiatric consultation at once.* Further, because the mood of some suicidal patients lifts when they finally decide to commit suicide, the family should not take an apparent improvement at face value.

Manic patients present different difficulties for the family, since the patients do not perceive that they are ill or showing impaired judgment. Frequently, the family must intervene to prevent the manic from shortsighted, self-destructive acts. Such family intervention may result in considerable friction. The sooner the manic patient can receive appropriate treatment, the greater the possibility that the family can avoid such turmoil.

Psychological Management of Depression

Although we believe that for major biological depression, medication is the immediate treatment of choice, psychotherapy is of value in several circumstances. In mild depressions, particularly those that seem related to life stresses, psychotherapy is often a useful initial treatment (if a complete psychiatric diagnosis has apparently ruled out biological depression). It is also helpful as a supplementary treatment directed at the psychological consequences of severe depression.

Psychotherapy for Depressive Reactions to Life Stress

As we have pointed out, mild depressions can also be biological in origin, but sometimes they are normal human reactions of sadness and grief to unavoidable experiences of loss or disappointment. In distinguishing depressive illness from ordinary sadness, the psychiatrist watches for such symptoms of depressive illness as loss of pleasure, appetite and sleep changes, energy loss, low self-esteem, and guilt.

The diagnosis is not made strictly in terms of the depth of the depression, because depressive illness can be either severe or mild, and the same is true of sadness or unhappiness resulting from unsatisfactory or tragic relationships with family, friends, and employers. Mild depressive *illness* responds best to medication, while even prolonged depression resulting from life's misfortunes may do poorly on antidepressant medications. Such sadness of circumstance responds to time, to change, and, in some instances, to psychotherapy.

Such psychotherapy should not be lengthy, and there is some evidence that the particular type of psychotherapy is not of great importance. Although many forms of psychotherapy claim success in dealing with depression, few have been studied intensively by means of recognized scientific procedures. In a recent, elaborate research investigation of the effects of psychotherapy and medication on depression, the two forms of psychotherapy studied—known as cognitive therapy and interpersonal psychotherapy—were found to be equally effective, and not significantly better than simple support. Other forms of psychotherapy may work similarly, but they have not been studied as carefully.

Cognitive therapy focuses on the depressed patient's distorted view of himself and the world, and interpersonal psychotherapy focuses on current relationships and behavior. Conceivably, psychotherapies that emphasize friendly support, or unconscious guilt, or reliving stressful events—to mention just a few of myriad possibilities—would do as well in helping the sad person to live through his painful episode. With any psychotherapeutic approach, if the patient is not feeling appreciably better by a maximum of three months, it is a good idea to get another consultation. The patient's problems should be reevaluated and the possible usefulness of medication considered.

Psychological Therapy for the Patient Successfully Treated with Medication

The fact that medication is of clearly documented, specific effectiveness in depressive illness does not imply that additional psychological treatment is of no value. Even when responsive to medication, the depressive patient may have lingering symptoms that are complications of the illness itself, sometimes with contributions from personal limitations and life stresses. In many instances patients will benefit by a combination of medication, psychological therapy, training in new social habits, and possibly even a change of lifestyle.

A frequent psychological consequence of depressive illness, particularly if the depression has lasted for a long time, is demoralization. Demoralization refers to the feelings of ineffectuality, inadequacy at solving problems, and inability to control one's life that stem from the biologically produced depression. The depressed person lacks drive, motivation, and the ability to face the challenges posed by complex personal problems—all as a result of the biological illness. Countless marital and other personal problems often develop as a result of depressive and manic-depressive illness. Serious marital problems probably occur in at least half of the couples in which one member is manic-depressive. In such situations, couple therapy or family therapy focusing on such problems may be of benefit.

Psychological problems produced by the illness frequently outlive the illness itself. They are not neurotic problems. They are not the result of the person's incorrect perception of the world and himself. They are the realistic consequences of his former inabilities. A medical analogy might be a treated broken leg. After the bone is healed and the cast is removed, the patient may have to exercise his leg before he can walk normally again. Although the bone is no longer fractured, the muscles have weakened and must be used to regain their former strength. Just as weakened muscles are a physiological complication of such an injury, demoralization is the psychological complication of depression.

The demoralization produced by depression often disappears with time, especially in the presence of fortunate life experience. However, psychological therapy may accelerate the process. A variety of other psychologically potent forces can also help, such as patient support groups, religious groups, social organizations, consciousness-raising groups, and encounter groups.

Self-Monitoring of Depression

A patient with depressive illness or mania should learn to monitor his own mood. The patient usually sees a physician once a week while medicine is being started or adjusted, but after that, visits become less frequent. Therefore, the patient should learn how to determine if he is getting better or worse, in both his feelings and his behavior.

Toward this end each patient should learn his own "target symptoms." Each individual patient does not necessarily have all the symptoms seen in depression and mania. Accordingly, two people may both have profound chemical depressions and yet have only some symptoms in common.

For example, both may have no zest for life—they may have lost interest in their usual activities and they may often feel sad and even suicidal. However, one may feel guilty while the other does not; one may sleep twenty hours a day and the other four; one may eat compulsively and gain considerable weight whereas the other has a marked loss of appetite and loses weight. One may be agitated and constantly in motion, while the other moves slowly as if stuck in molasses. The first patient may skip from subject to subject, whereas the other's mind may move so slowly that she forgets her first sentence by the time she has completed her second. The same variation occurs in mania. One manic may seem fine and act as if ecstatically happy, while another may be extremely irritable and angry.

In order to evaluate himself properly and to help the physician to evaluate his progress, the patient should learn his own target symptoms—that is, the particular symptoms he gets when depressed or she gets when manic. Armed with this knowledge, both the patient and the physician can tell when the depression or mania is improving or when—say, in a period when the patient has stopped taking medicine—the first mild but important warning symptoms appear.

Many psychiatrists will ask a depressed patient how he feels on a one-to-ten scale—with one as the worst ever and ten the best. While depressed the patient is likely to assign himself an unrealistically high number—that is, to report that he is much closer to normal than he really is. When medication and therapy have restored his mood to normal, he sees that his previous reports have been inaccurate. This is because each time the patient is in the middle of a depressed episode, he cannot remember exactly what it was like to feel good. When he receives effective treatment and returns to his normal mood, he is surprised how good it is to feel normal.

It is somewhat helpful to report to the physician that one is better this week than last, but one can feel better and still not be functioning very well. The real question is how the patient is doing in objective, descriptive terms. How much time is she spending in activities that she usually enjoys—gardening, bowling, refinishing furniture?

How much time is he spending fishing, playing chess, finishing the basement, or participating in the men's softball league? Although people can judge fairly well whether they feel better or worse from week to week, depressives forget not only how good they *feel* but what they *do* when normal. This is the best way of assessing change for the better or worse.

Although the symptoms of depression and mania are to a great extent inside the patient's head, many of the symptoms are clear-cut enough to be visible to an outsider. This means that other people can be helpful in determining the patient's progress or lack of progress. For example, a depressed patient may report that his interest in life is returning and that therefore he is well on his way to normality, but his spouse can tell the examining physician how the patient's interests still differ from his previous ones.

Similarly, the depressed patient is often quite unaware of his behavior and how it appears to others, but his family notices unusual tensions, irritability, withdrawal, and lack of affection. The manic's self-observation is often much less accurate than that of the depressive, for the illness itself makes him feel good, think well of himself, and be optimistic about his future accomplishments. Mania is associated with impulsive, ill-considered relationships. Many patients will devastate their lives personally, vocationally, and financially in a relatively short time before they acknowledge that they may be ill, but the spouse or other family member invariably notices the faulty functioning far earlier. However, one caution is necessary: when manic-depressive patients who are depressed begin to recover, they may "overshoot" and become hypomanic. Everyone around them may be so pleased with the disappearance of the depressive symptoms that they fail to perceive that the patient now has the opposite face of the illness. It is important to recognize hypomania as a symptom of illness because of the severe difficulties that may follow.

Self-monitoring is important because even after a patient has responded well to treatment, his or her need for medication often fluctuates. On a constant dose, one patient may experience bouts of depression while another may experience periods of pleasant but potentially destructive highs. The treated person with a mood disorder is somewhat like a diabetic. The diabetic cannot chemically process ("metabolize") the carbohydrate and sugar in his diet and must administer the hormone insulin to himself in order to normalize his metabolism. However, the diabetic's optimum dose of insulin is dependent not only on the nature of his faulty metabolism but also on the type and amount of food he eats, his physical activity, and the presence of other illnesses. All these factors may require him to increase or decrease his daily insulin dose. The doctor must teach the patient to measure the effects of these experiences on his diabetes and to adjust his diet and medication accordingly.

Most biological psychiatrists do not assign such responsibilities to the depressed patient, either because the adjustments are more complex or because psychiatrists have been more conservative in this regard. However, the patient must realize that his or her need for medication may vary, depending on stress, illness, and personal experiences. On a fixed and apparently adequate dose of medication, his psychological motor may not run smoothly. It may sputter and miss even when it is warmed up. The patient must learn to observe these misfirings and communicate them quickly to the physician, who will help the patient to adjust his medication. This will minimize fluctuations in the effectiveness of treatment. Like many other medical treatments, treatment for depression can be very good but does require constant supervision and adjustment.

CHAPTER
6 How to Get Help

ONE OF THE confusing problems that a person with a depression or depressive illness faces is finding the right kind of therapist. Because therapy for various kinds of emotional disorders is offered not only by psychiatrists but also by psychologists, social workers, nurses, and pastoral counselors, it is difficult for the potential patient to decide who can best evaluate his needs and help him to plan treatment.

Who Is Most Qualified to Diagnose and Treat

As the preceding parts of this book have emphasized, the best and most up-to-date care for severe depression *requires* the following:

1. Appropriate medical evaluation, with particular emphasis on identification of any medical problems that may be producing psychological symptoms.
2. A full evaluation by a psychiatrist who is expert in biological approaches. This includes the determination of whether the patient currently has a depression, the identification of the type of depression, and the diagnosis of any other psychiatric illness that may also be present.

3. Appropriate use of available antidepressant medicines—singly or in combination, as required by the individual patient.
4. Monitoring antidepressant treatment and any other necessary medical treatment.
5. The determination of whether the patient needs additional psychological treatment of some kind.

At present, the only therapists qualified to provide all of these services are psychiatrists with adequate training in biological psychiatry.

All psychiatrists are physicians who have attended four years of medical school and have had at least a year of postgraduate general medical experience plus three years of special training in psychiatry. A psychiatrist who wishes to become a board-certified specialist must pass an examination administered by the American Psychiatric Association. However, a board-certified psychiatrist is not necessarily up-to-date in his field because physicians do not need to be recertified periodically.

Psychiatrists with biological training often specialize in the diagnosis and treatment of depression, manic-depression, and other biologically caused psychological difficulties. No formal training programs in biological psychiatry exist. Psychiatrists master the field as part of their general psychiatric training or, on their own, following their formal training. Until the past decade most training programs in psychiatry emphasized the psychological causes and treatment of psychiatric problems (these programs were often indistinguishable from those given in social work, clinical psychology, etc.). Thus, older psychiatrists generally have *not* had training in biological psychiatry. A substantial number have completely retrained themselves, but many have not. This is particularly true among the group of psychiatrists most firmly committed to the psychological treatment of psychiatric problems, such as the psychoanalysts. Many psychoanalysts, despite their training as physicians, are actively opposed to the use of medication as the primary treatment of psychiatric problems.

Many nonpsychiatrist physicians (e.g., internists, family practitioners, neurologists) have also begun to treat large numbers of depressive patients. Often depressed patients who have been referred to psychiatrists will not go, believing that psychiatrists treat only crazy people. They think that accepting such a referral will mean that they are much sicker than they had realized, and they believe that going to see a general physician instead will demonstrate their lack of serious mental illness.

Sometimes a general physician will treat depressed patients either because there are no competent psychiatrists with biological training in the community or because he has no confidence in the available psychiatrists who specialize in psychotherapy. However, for many general physicians, training in the diagnosis and treatment of depression has been only on the job. Others, particularly family practitioners, may have had a relatively brief period (three to six months) of training in psychiatry during their post-medical school training (residency). In our experience, general physicians vary tremendously in their skill in handling differential diagnosis, drug management, and psychological assistance for depression. Some deal with most routine cases with great ease and are quick to refer nonroutine cases to biologically skilled psychiatrists. Others do not recognize the possible complexity of depressive illness, approach all kinds of depressives in the same way, and provide inadequate treatment.

As time goes on, probably nonpsychiatrist physicians will become less able to master the diagnosis and treatment of depression and manic-depression because knowledge about these illnesses is increasing rapidly. For example, a professional abstract service, published monthly, was five or six pages long a few years ago. Now the publication is twenty-five to thirty pages in length.

Nonphysician therapists, such as psychologists, social workers, and pastoral counselors, are handicapped in treating depressive patients because of their lack of medical training. Although many have doctorates and postgraduate training, their education largely focuses on psychological and social factors in mental disorders. Minimal attention is given to the all-important biological factors.

Formal training in these professions has only recently begun to address the question of differential diagnosis in psychiatry. Psychotherapists who are trained in these disciplines have usually been taught that most emotional problems can best be treated by psychotherapy. In particular, they have not been taught how to distinguish depressive illness and manic-depression from psychologically produced depression. Finally, none are trained to dispense the medications most effective in the treatment of depression and are not legally qualified to write prescriptions.

Finding a Psychiatrist with Biological Skills

A logical way to begin looking for a biologically trained psychiatrist is to request a referral from one's family physician. If the physician has not had much professional contact with psychiatrists in the community, one can inquire of the state or district branch of the American Psychiatric Association (APA). The APA will give the inquirer the names of several psychiatrists practicing in the community. The names are given on a rotation basis, and the caller can ask whether the psychiatrist is board-certified. However, the APA will provide no evaluation of the psychiatrist's skill, areas of specialization, or interest and training in biological psychiatry.

Another especially good way to locate specialists in biological treatment of depression is to find out if any nearby university medical schools have a research and treatment clinic for depression (or mood disorders or affective disorders). Such clinics generally not only conduct research but evaluate new drugs and train young psychiatrists in the diagnosis and treatment of depressive illness. The level of expertness in these clinics is usually high, and they are often able to recommend not only their own staff but psychiatrists practicing in the community.

If the university medical school does not have such a clinic, it is sometimes helpful to ask whether any of the senior staff members of the department of psychiatry see private patients. However, physicians associated with medical schools are not necessarily better trained than physicians in the community. The odds are greater that a physician chosen at random is well trained if he is associated with a medical school, but many medical schools still emphasize the psychological approach to psychiatric problems. Preliminary discussion with any psychiatrist is essential in order to ascertain his or her treatment approach.

We wish to emphasize that many excellent biologically skilled psychiatrists in the community are not associated with medical schools. We refer patients to such psychiatrists all the time; some of them are in individual practice and some are in good private clinics that specialize in depression.

Many communities have community mental health clinics, which are supported by federal and state funding and which offer psychiatric services on a sliding-fee scale. The philosophies of the clinics and the expertise of their psychiatric staffs vary considerably. In some, evaluation is done by nonpsychiatrists. In others, all evaluations are done or reviewed by psychiatrists. Community health clinics have the advantage of lower fees, but the prospective patient must ask the same questions of them that he would of any private psychiatrist whom he would contact.

In addition to these avenues for getting help, several national organizations provide assistance. The National Foundation for Depressive Illness (NFDI) is a nonprofit organization whose aim is to educate the public about the symptoms of depression, to update professionals in their recognition and appropriate treatment of depression, and to support research in depression. (Address: P.O. Box 2257, New York, NY 10116. Telephones: 1–800–248–4344.)

The National Depressive and Manic Depressive Association consists of patients and families who try to educate the public about depression and manic-depression and to help prospective patients obtain adequate therapeutic help. The central branch responds to requests for help by referrals to convenient local branches that have lists of physicians whom their members have found helpful. It does not attempt to certify the excellence of the doctors; however, the association's recommendations, based on experience, are very useful. National Depressive and Manic-Depressive Association, (Address: Merchandise Mart, Box 3395, Chicago, IL 60654.) Telephone number: (312) 939-2442.

Meeting with the Psychiatrist for the First Time

In the first interview, which will probably take an hour or two, the prospective patient should ask the psychiatrist about his or her approach to therapy. In particular, it is vitally important to find out what the doctor's policy is regarding the use of medicine. An open-minded psychiatrist will not think that such questions are presumptuous and will not conclude that the patient is resisting recognition of possible psychological problems. If the psychiatrist does seem to resent such inquiries, we recommend that the patient seek another psychiatrist.

Before being seen in psychiatric consultation, the patient should prepare a detailed list of all treatments, including medications of any sort, that he has received for any medical or psychological conditions. The actual dates and dosages of medications are crucial for evaluating past treatment. Memory is unreliable with regard to such information. The patient must check with his physician or pharmacist to get the exact numbers.

It is also desirable to discuss openly how the progress of the therapy will be evaluated. An increasing number of psychiatrists now find this approach acceptable; some even draw up contracts with their patients specifying the duties of both participants, the frequency of the meetings, and the point at which progress will be evaluated in order to determine whether the treatment should continue. If progress is not apparent, or if in open discussion the psychiatrist acknowledges uncertainty, it is perfectly appropriate for a patient to request a second opinion, a consultation. This does not necessarily reflect on the competence of the psychiatrist. It is merely a recognition of the fact that no physician can know everything and that some patients' problems can be exceedingly perplexing.

Depending on the severity of the depression, the psychiatrist may see the patient initially twice a week for two or three weeks, then once a week for a few weeks, and so forth. The psychiatrist should also recommend some laboratory tests, such as medical screening and thyroid. Psychotherapy is not a necessary component of the treatment of biological depression, but the patient and doctor may wish to discuss it.

Second Opinions

How long should one stay in treatment that is not help-ing? Probably eighty percent of patients with a mood dis-order will respond to at least one of three drugs, if each is tried in adequate dosage for a minimum of six weeks. The degree of response may vary considerably. Some patients will experience complete relief of symptoms, others will have some decrease in symptoms, and about twenty per-cent of properly diagnosed and properly treated patients will fail to respond.

If a patient has received three trials of medicine of six weeks each and does not feel any better, he and his psy-chiatrist should discuss obtaining a second opinion. Many psychiatrists themselves call in a colleague at this point because they may be puzzled or wonder whether they have overlooked something.

The preceding discussion has assumed that initial treat-ment has been by a biologically trained psychiatrist. If a patient with the symptoms of major depression (loss of pleasure, loss of interest, loss of energy, etc.) has been in psychotherapy for over three months with a nonbiological psychiatrist or a nonpsychiatrist and has not responded, he or she should obtain a consultation from a psychiatrist who offers biological treatment. Even if the symptoms are unclear and the therapist cannot be certain that the patient is depressed, such a consultation is advisable. Any patient with manic symptoms should obtain a consultation with a biologically trained psychiatrist immediately.

Patients being treated with antidepressant medication by nonpsychiatrist physicians should probably seek a second opinion if (1) they have received two trials of medication of at least six weeks each and their depression has not responded; *or* (2) psychological problems seem to be a significant part of the depression; *or* (3) any symptoms of mania are present.

Some patients with depression, like some patients with hypertension, are extremely difficult to treat. With these patients, even a skilled physician may have to try several medicines singly and in combination before he finds a recipe that works for a given patient. It is hard for a patient to distinguish between a good physician who is systematically trying medicines and a poorly educated one who may be prescribing several in a nonsystematic way. It is sensible to request a second opinion after lack of response even though one cannot be sure that it will be helpful.

Psychotherapy for the Depressed Patient

As we discussed earlier, a patient who is receiving adequate and successful medical treatment for depression may still have several psychological difficulties:

1. Demoralization caused by the depression may remain, and it may or may not tend to disappear with time.
2. Realistic problems in the patient's life may require a combination of psychological therapy, training in new social habits, and even a change in lifestyle.
3. Learned psychological maladaptations often require psychological therapy.

Obviously, it would be best if there were a large number of professionals available who were trained in both the biological and the psychological management of depression. However, adequate training in both the biological and the psychological aspects of psychiatric illnesses is uncommon, which makes finding well-rounded therapists difficult for patients and for referring physicians and agencies. We ourselves, when asked to refer a patient for treatment in a distant city, often must ponder long and hard in order to locate appropriate psychiatrists. We do not have too much difficulty in locating a physician for a patient with a clear-cut biological depression or a reputable psychotherapist for someone with clear-cut personal limitations or maladaptations. But when the patient's problems are a variable mixture requiring careful biological *and* psychological evaluation, finding an appropriate physician can be very hard.

We would like to emphasize that in such instances, biologically trained psychiatrists often turn to the many well-trained nonmedical psychotherapists, recommending psychologists, social workers, or others who are equipped to do the necessary psychotherapy for depressive patients. Sometimes psychiatrists also recognize that patient support groups, religious groups, and social organizations can provide the necessary support for depressives with special psychological needs.

Conclusion

Psychology and psychiatry have long been the playground of speculation. During the past twenty years— unbeknownst to the average and even the psychologically sophisticated layperson—a compelling body of information has accumulated indicating that many mood disorders (both severe and mild forms of depression, and manic-depression) are biological illnesses whose most effective treatment is medical. At present only psychiatrists trained in biological methods are adequately equipped to diagnose and treat these depressive illnesses. Other professionals can contribute to the treatment, but the patient with depressive illness should have the initial advantage of skilled diagnosis and advanced biological treatment.

In closing, we would like to offer one last piece of advice to the depressed patient receiving therapy (who is like any other medical patient receiving therapy). It was a piece of advice—a "law"—dispensed by one of the grand old men of American internal medicine to his medical students and interns: "If what you're doing is working, don't stop—if what you're doing isn't working, try something else." Profound wisdom, simply stated.

Index